Community
Technology

Community Technology

Karl Hess

HARPER & ROW, PUBLISHERS

NEW YORK, HAGERSTOWN, SAN FRANCISCO, LONDON

Portions of this work originally appeared in the Washington *Post*.

COMMUNITY TECHNOLOGY. Copyright © 1979 by Karl Hess. All rights reserved.
Printed in the United States of America. No part of this book may be used or
reproduced in any manner whatsoever without written permission except in the case
of brief quotations embodied in critical articles and reviews. For information address
Harper & Row, Publishers, Inc., 10 East 53rd Street, New York, N.Y. 10022. Published
simultaneously in Canada by Fitzhenry & Whiteside Limited, Toronto.

FIRST EDITION

Designed by Stephanie Winkler

Library of Congress Cataloging in Publication Data

Hess, Karl, 1923–
 Community technology.
 Includes index.
 1. Community development, Urban—Washington, D.C.
I. Title.
HN80.W3H47 1979   309.2'62'09753   78–15828
ISBN 0-06-011874-1   79 80 81 82 83 10 9 8 7 6 5 4 3 2 1
ISBN 0-06-090689-8 pk   79 80 81 82 83 10 9 8 7 6 5 4 3 2 1

There is not a single large institution or organization in the world today that is satisfactorily performing all of the functions people have assigned to it. They are creaking, cracking, and even crashing under their own weight. Everywhere people sense that things are going to hell. Yet people themselves persist, contrive to survive, even make things better; and more and more they do all of those things with less and less direct reference to the major institutions.

People seem to be going one way, institutions another.

The largest of all institutions, the nation-state, maintains itself by sheer force in much of the world. Even where it is supposed to be supported popularly, the old enthusiasms wane. In America, fewer than a third of the eligible voters elected the last President. America's most recent war (usually the proudest activity of a nation-state) was a shambles. What more and more people seem to want most from their government is for it to go away—after, of course, handing out the particular favor which is seen as its only redeeming grace!

Churches sag at the institutional level and are revitalizing at the local level, in new sects, evangelisms, mysteries. The largest of the tightly organized churches, the Roman Catholic, is fracturing and sliding like a geological mass, with its adherents going their way, the papal leadership going another.

Cities, virtually all of them, seem to have reached limits of satisfaction having to do with size and the cost of that size.

New York remains the largest city—and also the most precarious, the most dubious, the most perilous. Size has not saved it. Size seems to have damned it. In cities where there seems to be a rebirth of confidence and possibility, there also is a rebirth of life in the smallest of civic units, the neighborhood.

Schools, failing all along the line, have also grown all along the line, with the one-room schools giving way to the town schools and those, more recently, giving way to the consolidated schools. The shiny new buildings and the conglomerated classes produced—what? A crisis in literacy and a few winning football teams. Now school bond issues have a tough time passing anywhere.

The police get tanks, helicopters, bullet-proof vests, and a lifetime subscription to the CIA. The muggers get bolder. The rapes go up. And nobody ever did bother to get some cops to watch the executives.

Hospitals glisten like the command modules of spacecraft. Rare and wonderful surgery is performed. Medical miracles keep making the headlines—and a long siege of an ordinary illness bankrupts people. Meantime, back at the lab, one group of scientists spends millions to research a medical cure for cancer while another group spends other millions proving that the major causes of cancer are environmental.

The Surgeon General condemns smoking. The Secretary of Agriculture helps stimulate tobacco farming.

Everybody condemns the Arabs when they raise oil prices—then say how shrewd a business deal it is for American companies to own so much of the world's largest oil producer, Aramco, in Saudi Arabia.

Ronald Reagan keeps talking about getting Big Government out of our lives, then drums it up for a military occupation of Our Panama Canal, higher defense budgets, and more freedom for government security agents to poke and probe and even shoot wherever they want.

Leftists condemn the government for every wrong from racism to genocide—and then propose that an even bigger government take over all productive facilities.

Industry and business, also grabbing for the claimed efficiencies of scale, have become so concentrated in ownership that just 2000 (1 percent) of the 200,000 American industrial corporations now account for about 90 percent of annual profits and about the same proportion of total assets. Yet, products are more and more seen as sleazy, and advertising depends on the rankest appeals to push products. The people who design and make them are increasingly bored silly and dissatisfied with what they do. Alcoholism, narcotic addiction, suicide, divorce, and sabotage rise as the production lines go faster.

Television, with its creativity captured by three commercial networks and one politically controlled public one, shifts back and forth between mediocrity and ho-hum while entertainers make in a year what poets, scientists, and farmers make in a lifetime.

Corporate farms replace family farms, crops are grown more and more in great area-wide clumps or even in separate countries (tomatoes in the Bahamas, asparagus in Mexico), famine stalks the earth, blights sweep the giant farms, and machines that have replaced farmers prove incapable of functioning with care and sense (as witness the corporate-scale farming of the Soviet Union).

Small business perishes, and with it freedom of enterprise, as conglomerate managements and agreements replace old-fashioned marketing. Product differentiation replaces actual innovation, and style dominates over serviceability or need.

Even neighborliness and friendship become gripped by the symptoms of growth, so that simple affection of people for each other is replaced by the new industries of introspection, meditation, faddish indulgences, singles bars, dating companies, and pleasure consultants.

Finally, the places where we live become simply real estate, places primarily for speculation. The good town is the growing town, even if the growth displaces the residents, scatters them to other centers, pays them well for property abandoned, then charges them even more for property to replace it. And, like a final blow to the old American Dream, the possibility of even having a house to live in is now said to be beyond the reach of most of us. Progress. Growth. Moving on. Growing up, and up, and up.

In pathology, one form of unlimited growth is known as cancer. To many a Chamber of Commerce unlimited growth is still called "progress."

Yet, people by themselves, not as parts of the institutions which lead the cheering for all this concentration and growth, people by themselves keep going elsewhere.

Some townspeople simply shut the door. No more growth.

Some young people declare that community, not success, is their goal. Small business is suddenly a countercultural phenomenon. Family farms are said to be the mark of "the new pioneers."

All of these matters are discernible in the ordinary course of things. They do not require scholarly research at least to see the outlines. The outlines of the discontents are ordinary table talk. So are the outlines of the simmering hopes and the shimmering dreams and the changes.

At the heart of it all lies what seems to me an inescapable observation: People feel vague and dissatisfied, troubled, when their work seems to have no meaning or to be just part of some interchangeable inexplicable machine; when their life shrinks into the confines of a single house or apartment; when neighborliness is lost; when all life seems compartmentalized, packaged, processed; when anonymity seems the name of the game and one's name becomes a number.

The equally inescapable alternative would be community, understandable work, friends, someplace to stand, a reason to stand up, and a certainty of being counted, of being heard, of being a recognizable and not an indistinguishable part of the whole.

It does not seem much to ask to be a whole person in a whole world. Yet the world would have to change to make that possible. Is it possible? I am convinced it is. Possible. Practical. Not pie in the sky, but something for here and now.

4

The two crucial elements are community and technology. A *place* in which and a *way* in which people can live peacefully, socially, cooperatively; and *tools* and *techniques* to provide the necessary material base for that way of living.

Communities, of course, are human work; they arise from human decisions and interactions. But what about technology, knowledge, knowing how to do things and making the things with which to do them? They are seen so commonly as the results of institutional arrangements that viewing them as community enterprises requires what may seem a shocking reassessment. This book is for people who want to at least consider such a reassessment. For any who do, there is an initially comforting thought. You, we, are not alone. Thinking about community and thinking about the technologies appropriate to community is something people are doing in increasing, if not yet overwhelming, numbers everywhere on earth.

Most are not impelled by ideological furies. They are doing it for a simple and very decent, very human reason: there really doesn't seem to be any other way to go these days. All of the grand theories of central authority, of pyramids of power, ideological purifications, growth, bigness, and progress have been tried. Yet here we are, knowing that things just aren't working.

Because this is a book about technology which has very personal dimensions, it requires a personal statement at the beginning. Unfortunately, it is likely to sound outrageous. If it does, please understand that it derives from experience and not from ideological frenzy.

Like most of us, I have worked very hard and very long under the impression that the bigger anything is the better it is. I have worked very hard and very long under the impression that success is money, that time is money, that progress is money, that money is wealth. You know all of these things. We grow up knowing these things. In fact, *when* we know these things we are said to have grown up.

We see technology as a tool to do it all, to make things bigger, to make more money, to save more time. And we see technology as a way of accomplishing everything, as an entire way of thinking. With the time we save we have leisure—and with the leisure we have new technologies of recreation. When the recreation palls, we have new technologies of introspection and analysis to discover why it palls and, in effect, to provide a new recreation to fill all that time that we saved—but which, come to think of it, we are too rushed to enjoy. Perhaps then we turn to the technologies of narcotic tranquillity.

Above all, we see technology, most of us, as something remote, another product, built in another factory—something we can buy. Like food. Like satisfaction. Like respect.

I am convinced now that there are other possibilities. I have worked enough at the practical development and deployment of them to see them as wholly available as alternatives here and now.

It is possible for us—working together in social situations of various sizes according to our preferences—to spend our time almost exactly as we want to. The rules and imperatives that conventional wisdom fasten on us are not binding except to the extent we let them be.

Technologies, ways of working, kinds of tools, can be developed, deployed, and maintained at the community level.

Communities, founded upon ways of life that reflect the values and aspirations of the people who compose the community, can take long steps toward exactly the degree of self-reliance that will best serve the purposes of the community. Communities can, without complex social controls, cooperate with other communities to provide things not locally available, to enlarge cultures, to do anything that will enhance the community without destroying it.

There are no shortages of anything on the face of the earth that would prevent any community from surviving healthily and happily. If you say, Aha, there are shortages of petrochemicals so severe that not everybody can have them, the obvious answer is that not everyone needs them. There are other fuels. There are other chemicals. Petrochemicals seem essential not because of technology so good that everyone must

6

have it but because of technology so poor that it has become inflexible, dependent, stultified. The petrochemical industry is a monument to the folly of putting all our technological eggs in one huge basket. That huge basket is corporate and state domination of technology. This book is an argument for community participation, with all of the diversity and resultant flexibilities that that implies.

Technology, to hear most public descriptions and discussions of it, is concerned solely with great institutions: National Strength, Corporate Progress, Gross National Product, National Security, State of Knowledge.

You can practically hear the trumpets blaring and see the thrones of power glistening at the end of majestic red carpets. Ta-ra, ta-ra.

So long as technology actually seems that remote and that majestic, it will not serve us. Like a monarch, it will rule us. Rather, those who manage it will rule us.

The fact is that technology is simply the way we use tools, actual tools in the material sense, and tools of knowledge in the sense of skills and craft and technique. It is not majestic. It is quite earthy. It is not remote. It involves us all. It involves shopkeepers in crowded cities. It involves farmhands. It involves kids. Everyone. People here. People around the world. We are all tool users and knowledge users, from the tribal farmer scratching a seed furrow with a pointed stick to the high-energy physicist aligning a particle accelerator, from the shaman to the molecular biologist.

Science is another matter. It is a process: one way of observing the natural world, conjecturing about relationships in the natural world, rigorously testing those conjectures, and then making predictions as to performance and occurrence on the basis of those tested conjectures. It is also the process by which, over time, virtually every conjecture, even after acceptance, has been replaced by another. Science is a way of thinking. Technology is a way of doing work. Science is when someone, on the basis of a long-tested theory or conjecture, predicts that it will take so much energy to drive a certain nail

7

into a certain piece of wood—other scientific probing having established descriptions for energy and for the hardness of wood. Technology is when someone attaches a dense material such as metal, to a hand-suitable material such as wood, tubular steel, or fiberglass to produce the hammer that will impart the arm's energy to the nail (a device that involves another technology, based on scientific notions of friction, which is a theory, and so on and on).

Today, both science and technology are part of a public schizophrenia that is as deranging as the private kind

On the one hand, virtually all politicians and managers of great economic power, such as the Rockefellers, the Morgans, the Du Ponts, and the Fords, seem to regard science and technology as twin goddesses lighting the sky for the greater glory of capital expansion and the empire of businesses around the world. Socialist politicians and businessmen, or ministers of this or that as they prefer to call themselves, share exactly the same respect for science and technology and for exactly the same reasons but with different labels affixed.

Socialists and capitalists alike, for instance, feel that National Strength is simply a function of National Defense, which in turn is just a derivative of the Nation's State of Technological Know-How. They also feel that no matter what the problem— pollution, for instance—there will someday be a technological cure; so, therefore, there really are no problems, just political priorities.

Counter to all that are the people who hate science and technology. They reason that science and technology got us into whatever fix we are in, can only get us in deeper, and should now give way to other ways of thinking and working in order to save our souls and our lives. They ascribe to science a way of thinking which obliterates human consideration. They ascribe to technology a way of working which obliterates concern for nature.

To make the point of this book, it is necessary to oppose both those views, the capitalist-socialist one and the hate-science-and-technology one.

The point is that there is no reason in nature, in organization, or in science and technology for human beings to lead secondhand lives, under second-party rules, in second-class communities. Instead, there is every reason, *if they choose to,* that human beings can participate fully in all the decisions that affect their lives, be responsible for their lives, and with other human beings live in precisely the communities suited to their capabilities and cares rather than bound to someone else's advantage or blueprint.

This hardly means a sort of reckless freedom of choice based only upon desire. It does not suggest wishful thinking as the basis of society. It is meant to suggest responsible capability as the basis. Freedom of choice thus based means that when people choose the shape of community they must also be prepared and be capable of building that shape. If the choice is made in freedom and if others enjoy an equivalent freedom, it means that the responsibility must be borne by those directly involved and cannot be fulfilled by denying freedom to others. Freedom of choice that suggests the freedom to deny freedom is, except for debating teams, an obvious travesty.

Freedom of choice otherwise just might be the death of a free society. If, as it surely has, freedom of choice has come to mean freedom to choose between already existing situations in the development of which you were not directly involved, then it does not reflect a free society at all but rather an ordered society.

Freedom to create would seem to me a better demand for a free society, even the necessity to create, the necessity to make choices by actually making actions rather than just by picking "products," whether social or concrete.

America today is a technologically backward nation. It has a lot of technology. But the technology is largely frivolous, serving corporate caprices.

The technology has become very much like the politics. There is a lot of it—technology and politics everywhere, in every nook and cranny of our lives, in every ticking second of our times. But the politics is frivolous too. It serves the urges of

9

the two major political parties, the egos of the principal players in them, and the big businessmen who pay for it all out of profits made from the use of the technology!

The situations really do go together. The kind of technology that is possible, and which would suit the old yearnings of the American Dream, is exactly the kind that would undermine the sort of spectator-sport politics we have come to play. It would be a technology in which ordinary people participated very actively. It would be a tool to serve their purposes and make possible the kinds of lives they (and not Madison Avenue fantasists) want to live. Having a role in the development, deployment, and maintenance of technology, wouldn't people also want more of a role in politics? Wouldn't they want a politics that makes possible a democratic life rather than a politics that makes necessary a life subordinated not to politics but to *politicians?*

In politics a person is not a citizen if the person's only function is to vote. Voters choose people who, in turn, act like citizens. They argue. They establish the forms within which people live their lives. They make politics. The people who merely vote for them merely make politicians. People who argue for their positions in a town meeting are acting like citizens. People who simply drop scraps of paper in a box or pull a lever are not acting like citizens; they are acting like consumers, picking between prepackaged political items. They had nothing to do with the items. All they can do is pick what is. They cannot actively participate in making what should be.

In technology there is the same thing. To be merely a consumer of technology is always to accept and take what is and never to shape what could be.

Invention, science, the arts, civil life—all can be enjoyed at smaller levels of social organization, at the community level. Much of the best we have ever enjoyed in all those fields comes from small, not large, arrangements of work, research, education, and society.

Personal security, that great hobgoblin which often scares people into giving up freedom for some claimed increase in safety, can actually be provided more satisfyingly and more surely at smaller levels of arrangements, particularly at the community level. Even the security of a major geographical area, covering literally thousands of communities the size of a modern nation-state, could be provided in a military sense at a level of organization perhaps a tenth as great as the one which today threatens to engulf us in a regimented society without the enemy having fired a shot or issued an order.

I make an assumption in all this: *Most* people would prefer to live in a social setting where they know their neighbors, enjoy their work, and have a full voice in discussing the terms under which the work is done and the living is lived. I have another assumption that attaches to that: Such arrangements are structurally impossible in some social organizations. The point at which the scale changes is simply the point at which the purposes of all the people involved or the purposes of the institution and its institutional leaders become dominant. Numerical size is no gauge to this. A Spanish trade union, the CNT, with a membership of a million, once had only two paid employees. The purposes of the members dominated. On the other hand, in some very small communities, a single family or company may totally dominate. Generally speaking, however, sheer scale does at least tilt things toward command and away from democracy.

There is an obvious problem in imagining that the purposes of any group of people, large or small, ever will be so constant as to enable agreement and community. I for one do not imagine any such constancy. The individual purposes and predilections of people in a community are kaleidoscopic. However, if a *basic* purpose of the community is to be a community, and if there is shared respect for the neighbors and the neighborhood, then the multitude of other differences can be and will be argued and resolved without tearing apart the founding purpose. In short, it is the purpose of the community that undergirds the proposition, not any supposition that there won't be differences. If, of course, the differences ever become so powerful that they challenge the under-

11

lying purpose, so be it. The community is then upon a reef and might well have to split apart in order to disengage. But then all you have is two communities, each still presumably united at bottom by the same purpose as the old one—to have a community of shared respect!

Another way of putting this is geometrically. If the organization, regardless of numerical scale, is organized like a pyramid, with power running down from the top, and obedience as the base, then the administrative scale is big, a larger number of people controlled by a smaller number. If the shape is spherical, with power adhering to all of the particles in it, and with no way to establish an up-and-down order, then the scale is small, with decision-making involving the smallest of *all* social units, the individual, all of the individuals.

After the assumption that people do indeed want to live in a community, rather than anonymously in some sort of social conglomerate, the remainder of my arguments are not assumptions but practical propositions. They are not based upon things that lie in the future, on tools not yet discovered or used, on principles yet to be spelled out: They are based on what we have and what we are today.

Still it seems discordant. If possible and practical, why not present and palpable? If it isn't just dreaming, then why does present reality seem so immutable?

No doubt about it. There is, in any discussion of what could be, an overwhelming sense of things as they are—and powerful variations on the theme.

I often find myself asking why something isn't done differently only to hear the answer that:

1. There are rules against it.
2. That's not the way we do it.
3. Human nature just doesn't work that way.
4. It costs too much.
5. It's too simple (meaning my suggestion, of course).
6. It's too complex (meaning the thing being questioned, of course).

7. You just can't, that's all.
8. Well, I can't explain why not, but that's the way it is, and, besides, if I have to explain it you wouldn't understand anyway.
9. People just can't do things like that on their own
   a. Because they don't want responsibility.
   b. Because they aren't smart enough.
   c. Because they'd rather watch TV.
   d. Because "they" won't let them.

Reality is defined in all of those propositions as "the way things are" in a purely administrative sense. None of those propositions, not even the one about human nature, describes any hard-and-fast material reality.

Rules are made by people. People can change them—and not necessarily the same people who made them.

The way things are done is often a result of habit, custom, or old rules. Habits can be broken, custom that is not based upon some material imperative can be changed.

Cost is a bookkeeping matter, it is the result of social agreements and is not a part of the natural or material world. Costs are what a particular value system says they are. Paying as much for a painting as for the saving of a life is the result of a particular value system, always susceptible to change, and not the result of something handed to us by nature, physics, chemistry, biology, botany, physiology, or even psychology. One person's priceless psychological security is another person's wasteland.

Simplicity is not necessarily a curse. In the natural world simple rather than complex answers are more the rule than exception. It would be incredibly complex to ask the human mind consciously to direct the functioning of all the bodily parts, even though it might be satisfying to a certain managerial urge. On the contrary, the vital organs and the cells generally operate pretty much on their own, doing their jobs so long as they can without hierarchical structuring and coercion.

Photosynthesis (which simply is) is a lot simpler than having

13

the federal government or General Motors try to create nourishment from scratch.

Complexity, on the other hand, is by now a familiar managerial defense against anything in which there is a suggestion that people generally can understand, operate, or change any process controlled by someone who wants to keep the controls firmly in hand. (One reasonable response to a claim of complexity is to ask for clarification.)

The imperious "you can't" is just that, an exercise of authority and not of reason. It is a part of reality in about the same way the Inquisition was a part of religion. Again, it may be a "real" force, but it is a force that emerges from human purpose—which is changeable—rather than a material or natural imperative which might not be nearly so flexible. (It is possible by an exercise of human purpose to stop using petrochemicals as fuel. It is not possible by an act of human purpose to extend the availability of such chemicals beyond their actual availability in the natural world.)

Things that cannot be explained are things that cannot be explained and need not detain anyone interested in reality unless that interest focuses entirely on the inability of some people to say what they mean.

The idea that people can't, won't, or never have done something because most people are this way or that sometimes seems at least rooted in reality, unless you begin to recall that people have, over time, acted in so many different ways and have, even over short times, changed in so many ways as to seem to have almost limitless possibilities. Certainly there is nothing to suggest that their ways of working and living together are inscribed irrevocably in their DNA. If so, we could scarcely discuss the matter at all.

The most acute part of my own reality problem lies in the suggestion that "they" won't let there be any change. We all define "them" differently, of course. I am prepared to admit, as fervently as you wish, that there are some people who have mighty interests against letting anything change and whose

14

very life-styles are founded upon putting down any upstart suggestions that might set the applecart to wobbling. Some welfare recipients or pensioners can be understood as not wanting anything to change because of a cynical conviction that it would just get worse. The Rockefeller family hardly seems eager for change in the world, unless it is simply a reinforcing of the vast system of wealth which is their own welfare system, making it handily unnecessary to work except as whim dictates.

But, understanding that to be a part of reality is a shallow thing if it is not accompanied by a deeper appreciation of a reality in which all the idlers on earth—to continue with that example—do not amount to any great numerical shakes. The reality is that when most people want something to change it will change. A few muttering malcontents could scarcely stop it, particularly if the muttering comes from people who are clearly not among the most energetic or creative but actually the least, as is the case of the idle rich or the given-up poor.

Much of the criticism leveled against this book will call it "unrealistic" dreaming.

Accepted. If the real world is only the world of administrative decision, then I do have a reality problem and am properly disregarded as a simple ass braying in a distant boony. If, however, the real world is based not altogether upon desire but also upon material reality—and what we know of it, such as physics and chemistry, etcetera, and what we think of it, such as poetry and philosophy—then administration may be seen as merely one sort of effective opinion and not a "law of nature" after all.

If that is the case, and this book will try to make it, then the criticism of these speculations as unrealistic should be changed to saying that they are merely unpopular. And that in turn might be modified by saying, Unpopular right now but maybe not tomorrow.

Local liberty is the heart of community. A community without liberty is just a bunch of people living in the same area—a sort of arrangement all too familiar in the suburbs, for instance.

The community without liberty must accept what is given. Its boundaries are not merely geographic, they are legalistic, even cultural. Some power outside of the community is in control.

Take one of the slick, sleek new planned communities. They are prepackaged, processed, and perfected before anyone moves in. The mix of incomes has been set by the range of prices or rents. The paths, byways, stores, working places—even the mood produced by architectural styles and building placement, by wooded areas, water, and recreation—all have been established. People do not move in to form a community, to be part of a community of their own contriving; they simply move in. What is meant to pass for community is already there, planned and put into place by people who need not live there.

A community that richly reflects the aspirations, capabilities, and social agreements of the people living there would, by definition, have to be one they built, one in which there is the liberty to make the community and not just move into it. After the building there must be the liberty to maintain or change it as the successive generations of the people involved decide. That process thrives best where the community was founded in liberty. It starts a good habit. Made-to-a-mold places do not.

16

The disappearance of community, particularly in city life—where neighborhoods once were strong communities but where only a few still survive—involves points which are popularly made against neighborhoods and against community.

Small-scale social organizations, such as neighborhoods or other community structures, are said to be inefficient, they are said to be unable to provide civil rights (or unwilling to), and they are said to be impractical in purely material terms.

The argument of efficiency has already fallen of its own bureaucratic weight and is taken seriously only by those desperately hanging on to traditional power, such as the politicians of New York City or, for that matter, of all other megacities.

Efficiency arguments once included every phase of civil life. It was supposed to be cheaper to have a big city than a little one because the administrators could purchase supplies in such large and economical batches. But the cost of the purchasing process itself and the cost of storage and the cost of distribution have begun to wipe out the claimed savings.

Large police forces were thought to be more efficient and effective than small ones. Today in most major cities the most innovative and the most familiar changes in police forces are those which return the individual patrolmen to neighborhood beats and which try to establish precincts as parts of neighborhoods. The most highly praised force in the country, that of Los Angeles, has made neighborhood emphasis the central theme of crime prevention and detection. An in-depth study of citizen reaction to police organizations made at Purdue found the clearest evidence that people prefer police organizations which are close rather than remote, scaled to fit into the community rather than scaled to stand over it. And even though the FBI's justly famed crime laboratory is clearly a central facility, the bureau's skill at what it does most usefully, catching ordinary rather than political criminals, depends to a large degree upon its widely decentralized system of field offices, its neighborhood agents, you might say. And those field offices, in turn, operate most effectively when they do

17

not have to spend long hours catering to the whims of the central bureaucracy, as they often did in soothing the political rashes of J. Edgar Hoover.

Large-scale welfare systems, as common sense should have suggested at the very outset, can never operate as effectively as can a local charity—where needs are known, where caring is personal and not cool and remote.

Large-scale health facilities (sickness facilities, really) such as the great teaching hospitals can render spectacular care if a person is suffering from something interesting, yet may not have room for the person with a commonplace affliction. Also, the price of caring for patients in large facilities is all-of-a-kind, no matter the affliction, and that price is notoriously high. Already, the first rumblings of demand for a community-scaled localized sort of health care are being heard. Home care could, in fact, meet the needs of many patients, given a medical profession that was itself sufficiently decentralized and not drawn to the convenience of assembly-line hospitals—convenience, and easier profits.

Paramedics, nurses, the relatively new nurse practitioners with their advanced and specialized training, and other not-quite doctors also represent a useful and common-sense decentralizing influence in health care—and a direction toward community-scaled localized services. Such services, incidentally, need not, without other cause, mean the end of the large teaching hospitals. But they could indicate an important movement against the tendency of big hospitals to substitute themselves for *all* health facilities in a given area.

Educational efficiency is now farcical in terms of large-scale operations. The more money that has been spent on big buildings, the tinier the results in terms of well-rounded, literate children. The fact of the matter now is that large consolidated schools are often defended publicly more for their effectiveness in providing hot sports teams than for any educational reason. Education has moved from performance and productivity into the style of a spectator sport; what is done in the school is not as important for some people

18

(particularly those people of a booster or Chamber of Commerce mind-set) as what is seen. Looks are more important than brains in such a mind-set with, unfortunately, considerable justification. The Chamber of Commerce, in short, knows that other businessmen looking for a town will not be so much concerned with the true social character or possibilities as with the kinds of illustrations that can be put in a brochure to lure employees, who also will be felt to be tuned to style and fashion and surface appearance rather than to material reality. What business, for instance, would extol the value of an area's schools in terms of describing excellent individual teachers when it can simply choose to show a picture of excellent buildings? Style is, after all, the basis of much business—so why not the basis of social attraction as well? And, of course, it is.

It seems to me that the most powerful thing that the argument regarding the inefficiency of small-scale organization has going for it is the pervasive mood of consumerism in the country.

New consolidated schools, new towns, and most new prepackaged social offerings depend on a consumerist mood and mode. In fact, the major argument overall for favoring big organizations over small ones is that the big ones do make it easier for people to be passive; that is, they depend on delivering entire life-styles and not just single products. People are said to desire this. In this perception, progress is in part the ability to escape "doing" things (action) so that people can have or enjoy things (objects).

The new town, in its most flamboyant modern form, does not simply say as did older subdivisions, Come here to buy a house; it says, Come here to buy a way of living, a way already defined and extolled in four-color brilliance. One town may be for the "modern couple," another for "young families," another for "the man on the way up," still another for "the leisure years." The automobile makers do not say, as did the elder Henry Ford, Here is transportation that you may buy; they say, Here is an entire self-image to buy, one which, incidentally, provides transportation when the traffic isn't too heavy. Buick Skylarks, for instance, are for "free spirits"; Cadillacs are for those who have "arrived."

Television is a notable example and in all probability a notable contributor. Radio skits and sketches used to provide information and suggestions, but the listener had to provide the context and the texture in his or her own mind. Television, as the American philosopher Marcus Raskin has put it, actually colonizes that inner refuge of the person, the person's own dreams, packaging and processing an entire image structure for people who, if they wish, may simply consume visually an entire world of action. And they need never move. Or act. They can just be.

In great cities where neighborhoods have vanished, passivity applies to most phases of life except moving from one consumed entertainment to another. Neighborhood life, by contrast, has traditionally been a structure woven from the participating activities of everyone on the street, from the hawkers of wares and the conversational clumps, to the watchers at the windows, to games, art, and celebration.

There is about a small-scale organization an overall emphasis on productivity rather than consumption. The nonproductive stand out more sharply, if nothing else. The person who will not be part of local life cannot enjoy the easy anonymity of a faceless, larger social setting. It does not mean that a person may not in a neighborhood be totally withdrawn. It just means that there is general awareness of the withdrawal, which certainly seems fair to the neighborhood as a whole and certainly is not unfair to the person who has withdrawn. It might be unkind in the minds of some, scarcely unfair. Only a hermit may reasonably expect anonymity. Curious, active people have no use for it.

Anonymity is one of those "rights" of large-scale social organization that has a double function. It keeps people compartmentalized, and thus at the mercy of the social organization rather than as cooperating actors in it. It makes it possible to evade responsibility, to be an isolated cipher in a social setting, to have at best a sort of hit-and-run relationship with the social world around one.

Another virtue of anonymity, so ingenious as to deserve attention, is that ascribed to it by the liberal journalist Henry Fairlie. In his moving and justly famed defense of the American supermarket as a pinnacle of human achievement, Fairlie points out that in a supermarket the consumer, guaranteed anonymity by the mass traffic, may indulge whatever food folly he or she may wish without drawing the attention of a buttinsky neighbor who might laugh, scoff, or scold. Fairlie does not trouble himself with examining the other side of that coin: that such anonymous, isolated, impulsive buying of foolish food also permits manufacturers to sell products that provide no nourishment, often are injurious, and would probably be laughed at or scorned out of town if ever discussed openly with friends and neighbors. But, most importantly, the foolish anonymous buyer is not so much exercising a right as simply buying a poor product. I don't question one's right to buy a foolish or dangerous product. I question a manufacturer's decency, ethics, and claims to be a part of the community in profiting from poor products.

From the anonymity-passivity position, finally, comes the basic canard against people delivered with smug assurance by the defenders of large-scale organizations. People, they say, do not *want* to do things for themselves, think things through for themselves, go to meetings, be part of a community, and so forth. People, they say, are sheer appetite. This does not include the people making the charge, of course. They are hardworking, responsible, eager for challenge, always wanting to do more. They are people, the implication is, while we are slugs. The woman to whom a TV ad says, You are what the shine of your dishes is, is being told this. The voter who is told that only by electing better leaders can things be accomplished is being told this.

And always the refrain: You are a consumer, somebody *else* is a producer. Production is not a community matter; it is an "expert" matter, best left to managers and politicians.

21

Materially and otherwise, that attitude is a deadly mistake. Discussion of the material side of it will occupy much of this book.

Productivity in community terms is a social activity, not always just a material one. People talking together are productive of a community of shared information. The watchers from the windows may be productive also of information that may be shared. Not to slight material productivity at all, but a major productive activity in a local setting *is* the sharing of information. It is one of the ways that a neighborhood stays aware of itself and thus stays a neighborhood. This may seem a praise of gossip. It is. Gossip is the news and the chronicle of the commonplace, the everyday, the shared information about what is going on where we are. It is not necessarily inaccurate, any more than any other type of information must be inaccurate. It can be, depending on the motives of the people involved; it can also be accurate and incisive, depending on those motives. However, to call what Walter Cronkite mouths "The News," as though there is no other, and to call the talk in a neighborhood mere gossip is to prefer life in the clouds to life on the ground. A major possibility in a free society, it seems to me, would be to reverse things so that the most important news would be the real news of real possibilities right where we live. News of other communities could be informative and helpful, but it would not be, as it is now, *the* news.

The consumerist aspect of so many large-scale organizations has an internal reflection as well. Inside of large-scale organizations after a time there seems an inevitable development in which people begin to succeed by being consumers instead of producers.

Successful junior executives consume, in effect, the styles of successful superiors, add to them ideas brought from fashionable consultants, and then advance on the basis of those consumed activities. The original executive—the one with an experimental mind and with experiments in mind, the producer—becomes the target of all the others, is seen as a great rocker of boats, and his every daring action is watched not for success but for failure. There is another way in which the large industrial and business corporations have themselves become consumerist in nature. They grow, characteristically, by acquiring, by consuming other successful and innovative organizations—smaller organizations. They do not grow by producing. They grow by consuming. They do not add new knowledge so much as they just add new mass.

The essence of consumerism is that those caught in its grasp behave as though the ability to purchase is in fact an ability, a manifestation of merit, of expertise, and, further, they behave as though what they purchase actually confers upon them real characteristics, actually defines them as human beings. We are, the consumerist credo goes, what we buy.

The official, or Nader, version of consumerism simply feeds the fire.

The Nader approach, no matter its decent motives, also sees people as defined by what they buy; it sees buying as the most significant activity of most people and thus feels that to protect their purchases is a major good.

The alternative, which is emphasized by a participatory community and by the sort of technology appropriate to it, is to see the human role of production as crucial and to regard the work people do as far more significant than the things they buy. In short, consumerism regards people as appetite; community regards people as creativity.

The argument against community in terms of efficiency, therefore, finally boils down to the components of efficiency itself. If efficiency is seen wholly in terms of satisfying the consumerist mode of human life, then the anonymous city (where a person may consume anything without appearing foolish or profligate to nosy neighbors) is a splendid milieu, the production-line factory a splendid workshop, and gadget-glitter technology a titillating glory. If, on the other hand, efficiency is seen as the way in which a situation reflects the creative mode, the community mode, the human being as active and not passive, then smaller-scale ways of living together and working together may be viewed as serviceable.

All of this reflects the difference between an overall concept of rights and of responsibilities. Rights are administrative; they are legal or even legalistic statements deriving from an institution of power. Responsibilities are perceived, necessary ways of behaving.

In nature there are no rights. No creature has a right to anything, no blade of grass, no anything. That is, all life in a material sense involves not the *rights* of creatures or cells but the *nature* of creatures, plants, cells. Cells behave in certain ways. They do not proclaim a right to do this or that; it is just what they do.

Human beings, no matter how complex an agglomeration of cells they may be, also have certain natural functions which cannot be modified by statements but are inherent and natural.

There is, in the natural order, no absolute right to life, to sustenance, to shelter, to anything. Human beings do not provide or produce any of those things by *right*. They produce them by *action*. They come from concrete conditions and actions. Part of the process, of course, may (and usually does) involve abstraction, analysis, and theory; but only the active application of those interior actions in the exterior world produces anything—poems, philosophy, gears, wheels, or transistors.

Take a person in the wilderness, or alone in a room. The person has no rights at all. It may be said that he or she has a right to live. But that right cannot be exercised except by action. The person, or some person, or some something has to do something. Otherwise, if the person in the wilderness will not pluck a berry, the person will starve. If the person in the room will not call out, will not move, that person will starve. And the room, incidentally, could not have been built by a proclamation of right, it had to be built by an application to materials of energy and knowledge.

Yet we know that there are rights. Everybody talks about them. Precisely. Rights derive from talk, from human talk, from human agreement. All rights are social in nature. There can be purely theoretical rights, of course. They exist in a

24

person's head. They cannot exist outside of that head except by talk and by agreement—or by force.

Happily, there are ancient agreements about rights. The common law represents such an ancient agreement regarding such things as the right to protect oneself against murder and theft and the right to punish those who violate that right. Constitutions like that of the United States represent, if not ancient agreements, at least respectable elderly ones. Yet, in every constitution that provides for judicial interpretation (actually it can also be reinterpretation) of the constitutional agreements, there is copious demonstration of the fact that those rights are not only what people generally say they are but they are most forcefully exactly what *some* people say they are. In this, the most palpably free nation-state on the face of the earth, that is nevertheless an obvious fact of civil life. Rights today are what the state says they are. If or when rights are seen as what people *other* than the leaders say they are, the occasion is known as a revolution.

Revolution, as most familiarly defined by today's right and left, is the substitution of bosses, one for another. Their revolutions seek to maintain the system of top-down leadership, of elite control of the masses, citizens, or whatever you call them. They seek only to change the personnel at the top.

Some, of course, are benevolent, even kindly. Candidates for the American presidency speak of leading the people, through hard times for instance, to a brighter tomorrow. Commissars just lead; they don't have to explain.

Benevolent or malevolent, the top commands; the rest follow or at least are expected to.

Could it be otherwise? Doesn't someone always *have* to lead? Don't most people want to follow? Isn't it more efficient that way? Isn't it, in fact, the way things have always been, part of human nature?

The answers, I think, are yes, no, no, no, and no.

In arriving at the answers, the question of scale becomes, to me, crucial. The scale at which people can participate in making the decisions that affect them is a scale acceptable to

25

and nourishing of a free society. Scales beyond that just naturally are conducive to, at best, representative forms, in which the most one can hope for is a chance to pick someone to make the decisions. At worst, of course, even that choice is denied. But in either case decisions are made remote to the discussion of all the people affected.

The difference lies in whether or not we wish to live by coercing or exploiting others. To live by leeching off others requires some very strict social controls and arrangements. We have such arrangements and controls today. Under them, most people have to conform strictly to conventional wisdom and to conventional standards in order that a few—the ones who make the rules—can live pretty much as they wish. Yet even the people who make the rules are to an extent constrained by them. The masters and the slaves always have been chained one to another in some way.

A different way of living is to live in freedom by cooperating with others so that the rules of your lives together are set by yourselves. If those are the terms under which you want to live, there is no *material* reason for you not to do so.

The rules and imperatives that conventional wisdom has imposed on us so far are not binding except to the extent we permit them to be. We acquiesce to the rules, literally. Nature does not force us. We volunteer.

The scale at which goods that are needed for a healthy, pleasant life may be produced can be reduced to a community level.

If production can be reduced to a community level, so can social arrangement. Community, not nation or corporation, could be the basis of social life, permitting all those affected by decisions to be participants in those decisions. Democracy, which is often sacrificed for imagined efficiency, can be efficient as a way for people to live together, even if it is cumbersome.

It is possible for people in their communities to develop, to deploy, and to maintain the sort of technology, tools, aids, and techniques that will permit them to live as they wish—so long, of course, as they don't wish to live in a way that requires the coercion of others. Today's technology, in fact, works the other way. It permits a relative few to live the way they wish by fastening rules and regulations on everybody else. The executives of General Motors do not have to punch a time clock precisely because all of the people who design and make the products do. The Du Pont families can live pretty much as they please so long as all the people who could make a particular synthetic fiber behave as though the Du Pont family owns that particular combination of chemicals and that no one else is entitled to it without permission and so long as the people who buy the fiber believe that it is essential to their lives and that the only way to get it is to buy it.

Ways of living should and can reflect the culture of communities and not be established for communities by others. Again, the Morgans and the Mellons and the Rockefellers can establish precisely the ways of living they wish to enjoy in large part because they can also heavily influence the ways of living in other communities. The Rockefeller children can all go to private schools; the Rockefeller Foundation will spend millions making sure that the other children on the continent, if not the entire world, go to schools owned and operated by the nation-state and dedicated to the proposition that most children (excepting those of the rich and powerful) must fit into the way things are.

Communities, however, cannot exist apart from nature. They are part of nature, even though their location in the midst of cities sometimes obscures the fact. A major way in which humans relate to the natural world is through technology—the development and use of tools to utilize natural resources for human purposes. A neighborhood needs technology exactly appropriate to its scale of social organization and to its human purpose. If a neighborhood is totally dependent on outside institutions for technology it will be shaped in large part by the purposes of those institutions rather than by the purposes of the neighborhood's citizens.

The need for neighborhood people to become involved in

technology is similar to the need of neighborhood people to become involved in social and political action. The first step is to demystify the subject. In politics this means demystifying the idea that "they" always must do things. In fact, "we" must do them. In technology this means demystifying the idea that all technology is beyond ordinary understanding and that neighborhood people must simply accept what "they" give us. Again, we must begin to produce our own. This includes even science itself, the discovery of the principles upon which technology is based, as in such American ideas as the colonial associations in which craftsmen supported and engaged in scientific research. The prestigious Franklin Institute, whose members once supported Franklin's pioneering work on electricity, is an example. Today at the Institute for Local Self-Reliance basic research is being done by people in the neighborhood.

There is great difficulty, however, in convincing people that they can get involved with subjects that have for so long been deliberately obscured and made to appear too complex for local action.

A special point should be made about education. Young people in a neighborhood would be better served by apprentice training in neighborhood enterprises than by most present-day schools, where, instead of common-sense natural ways of thinking, they are afflicted by highly obfuscated and regimenting instruction.

The most powerful point to be made for community technology efforts is that when people take any part of their lives back into their own hands for their own purposes, the cause of local liberty is advanced; and such liberty, in turn, seems the strongest base on which to found a decent culture of mutual aid and humane purpose. In such a revolutionary change toward a free society of volitional social arrangements, liberty would have to be defined, agreed to, and made real locally, in communities. For that is where people live.

Local liberty has been attacked most specifically in political terms. Local interests are said to be too narrow for national goals. Local life-styles are said to be too disparate for national homogeneity. Local resources are said to be too uneven for national "fairness." People where they live are assumed to be untrustworthy. Thus politics becomes, and indeed is, the politics of *the world where people do not live:* the politics of international business and expansionism and the politics of abstract national goals.

Since this derives from political judgment, stemming from prevailing national political power, it is a judgment that can be reversed, altered, or simply forgotten. Local liberty, which was once an attractive opinion, could become an attractive opinion again—so long as it is considered, as with other politics, *just* a matter of opinion.

But are there areas of the concern that are *not* matters of opinion? Are there aspects of local liberty which are rooted in the natural and physical rather than social and political worlds?

Yes. Local liberty cannot be considered apart from the natural world. If local liberty has no material base, then it ultimately has no base at all. National political liberty—the freedom of national political leaders to act—has such a material base. For the generals it is the material base of nationally sponsored weapons production, which, in material fact, gives them the physical power to protect and extend political decisions. For the multinational corporations it involves continued access to raw materials upon which production may be based and flexibly moved hither and yon.

Unless localities could have an equivalent base in the material world, a base that can literally support the freedom of local people to make political decisions which affect their lives, then local liberty must remain a mere administrative proposal, gauged roughly by the amount of elbow room the local people are given by those who *do* have a base in the material world from which to exercise power.

At first glance, the prospects of a material base for local liberty seem so slim that it is understandable that arguments about it are usually political arguments, involving the convenience of higher power in "letting" some power rest at a local level.

As a matter of fact, so powerful has been the assumption that there is *no* base in the material world for local liberty that the development of political institutions has moved away from local liberty toward ever more centralized and remote power, despite the failures of centralized and remote political institutions. The remedy for the collapse of big institutions has been seen as simply the building of even bigger institutions. One important reason for this, I suggest, is that it is assumed that local liberty is simply *impractical* as well as being politically undesirable. In short, why try it when it is totally unrealistic? How could a neighborhood do what a city cannot?

The assumption is rash and uninformed. And, as are so many decisions in politics, the assumption is contrary to and even hostile to scientific knowledge and technological developments.

One seemingly sound base for the assumption, however, is the matter of food. A city neighborhood, seen as a concrete-bound ghetto, scarcely seems worth considering agriculturally. True enough. Agriculture and city spaces are apparently incompatible. Gardening and city spaces are not. Can gardening produce ample food for a neighborhood?

Hydroponic gardens in small greenhouse enclosures produce vegetables at a rate many times greater than ordinary agriculture. In one notable example, ten acres of greenhouses produced two million pounds of vegetables annually at a cost of twenty cents per pound, including the amortization of the structures, the desalting of water (it's a seaside operation at Abu Dhabi on the Persian Gulf), administration, etc. The most interesting point about such projects is that they can easily be subdivided, with the greenhouse becoming roof-sized and still yielding high growth in proportion to space allocated. City rooftop spaces, plus vacant lots or even the centers of streets, could be used to grow ample vegetables for a local population. The Institute for Local Self-Reliance, in Washington, D.C., maintains a good example. This is not to say that any neighborhood would not want to supplement local vegetables with those grown by other, distant communities. They surely might. And that in turn just means that neighborhoods also have an inherent capacity to engage in "foreign trade."

Herd animals such as beef cattle are clearly inappropriate to city neighborhoods. Chickens and fish are just as clearly appropriate. Aquaculture—growing fish in artificial settings—can produce high yields of high-quality protein in basement spaces. In one experiment undertaken by the author and associates, an inner-city basement space, roughly thirty by fifty feet, was sufficient to house plywood tanks in which rainbow trout were produced at a cost of less than a dollar per pound. In a regular production run the total number of fish that can be raised in such a basement area was projected to be five tons per year.

In these discussions of material aspects of local liberty, it is freely given that simply realizing a technological possibility does not make inevitable a social decision to adopt it. That remains a political and a cultural discussion. But—the decision to oppose local liberty or to adopt it *is* a decision. It is not a part of nature. The material base for local liberty does exist.

Problems of waste disposal also have undoubtedly contributed to the assumption that there is no material possibility for local liberty. A city waste sewerage system, indeed, would seem to defy any ability of a single neighborhood. At the very least it can be assumed—and, I feel, justifiably—that a neighborhood would have to join with all contiguous neighborhoods to duplicate or even maintain the usual city sewerage system. And having done that, it might be argued, why not let "nature" take its course and just stay together for all other purposes as well? Why bother about liberty? (That, of course, requires an answer in ethics. I will continue with emphasis on the material.)

City waste sewerage systems are wasteful, unnecessary, often dangerous, and certainly technologically backward. Neighborhoods are hooked into them because of history, not because of any current necessity. First of all, waste is not a problem, it is a resource. City waste systems simply ignore this. They waste the waste. In-house waste-digestion systems, now commercially available at costs as low as a thousand dollars, will convert all human and kitchen wastes into an odorless fertilizer. Some provide modest amounts of heating gas as they do it. (The average family could do all its cooking on the gas produced by its own waste.) Variations of waste-digestion systems for single dwellings could include processing plants to serve an entire neighborhood housed in an abandoned dwelling or the basement of an apartment house. The money used now to maintain, replace, and expand existing systems could be directly converted to the permanent solution offered by digestion systems. (Storm water, now carried through huge pipes to nearby streams, could instead be stored under a neighborhood or in a neighborhood "lake.")

Manufacturing today is thought of as a massive large-scale system by advocates of massive large-scale ownership.

It is assumed that it is appropriate to our needs mainly because of assumptions about those needs: quickly obsolescent products, package-emphasizing products, and proliferating fad products.

In point of material fact, manufacturing has undergone the

sort of technological change that has characterized all science-based activities in this century—a distinct tendency toward decentralization and small-scale units. A truly modern cybernated plant, turning out a vast array of machine parts, for instance, can be housed easily in a city neighborhood, in conventional office space. It uses computers to direct its tools, and can be handily operated by workers trained in the neighborhood. Transistors, the heart of electronics, are extremely demanding of material quality and specialized tooling-up but are also quite adaptable to small-scale local production. Plastics, which have got such a bad name because of their use in disposable containers, actually include some of the finest building materials known, permanent materials far stronger than steel, and they can be fabricated in small-batch operations. Even steel production has undergone a distinct shift toward smaller-scale facilities, such as continuous slab casting.

Raw materials, of course, are not usually appropriate to neighborhood production—city neighborhoods, that is. Most raw materials, however, are produced in such highly localized situations (a mine, for instance, or a group of oil wells) that it could be said they represent neighborhood-scale activities at a far remove.

If the raw materials are forever consigned to central buyers or to central governments, then their use as neighborhood resources will remain also at a far remove. There is no technically compelling reason, however, that the neighborhoods that produce raw materials could not trade those raw materials more directly with neighborhood refining facilities or with facilities maintained by groups of neighborhoods.

Energy production is strikingly adaptable to neighborhood scale. Solar energy, economically collectable as heat, could provide at least half of the cooling and heating requirements of any inner-city neighborhood. Photovoltaic cells that directly convert solar to electrical energy are on the verge of manufacturing breakthroughs that could make them the cheapest, most decentralizing power source yet.

Transportation within neighborhoods generally is seen as

merely an extension of the transportation demands not of citizens but of corporations. Yet the two demands are different. Corporate transportation need not occupy the total travel space of a neighborhood. Most citizen travel is of short duration and is ideally suited to electric vehicles. These vehicles in turn are simply built and also quite adaptable to the most localized production facilities. General Motors boasts that its Basic Transportation Vehicle can be built in a space the size of a barn and for a total capital investment of $50,000. Run by an electric rather than internal combustion engine, the BTV, or something like it, could serve most of the transportation needs of any American neighborhood. It could also be built there.

The most vital of city services, police and fire protection, have always been thought of as highly localized in nature. Firefighting facilities are not concentrated in some superfirehouse. They are spread as widely as possible, and the wisdom of this policy is rarely questioned. Police protection, when centralized and withdrawn from a neighborhood setting, as has now been widely recognized, results in disadvantages rather than economies of scale. A desire to return to neighborhood-based protection is evident in most cities. Central laboratory facilities for the police might not be economically duplicated in every neighborhood; but the matter has been given little study, and with an increase in local manufacturing skills there might not be as much difficulty in providing each neighborhood with its own microscope, computer-held files, and so forth, as might be imagined.

Health care, on the other hand, seems far more complicated, and the current tendency to destroy small facilities in favor of huge teaching-hospital empires might appear an argument against any consideration of locally based health care. At the same time, however, the common-sense emphasis on paramedical personnel to handle perhaps a majority of everyday health problems and the equally common-sense emphasis on citizen health awareness show a movement as strikingly toward localization as the more publicized movement toward megamedical centers. Although it is true that exotic ailments might not be treated in good style in a local medical facility, it is also true that most people do not require such service and that to distort an entire technology for the least rather than for the greatest needs seems a questionable practice.

Simply reinstituting the practice of house calls by physicians would, probably, eliminate the need for a majority of today's centralized medical facilities.

Communications and information systems are already involved in technologies which are adaptable without any question to the most localized uses. Virtually every neighborhood in America has within it amateur communications technicians of reasonably high skill: ham radio operators. Citizen-band radios further democratize the use of radio communications. Further, the very scale of the neighborhood makes it adaptable to communications of the most traditional kind—bulletin boards, wall posters, signs, even town criers or sound trucks. Newspapers on a community scale can be produced in small spaces and with wise recycling of materials or even substitutions of materials (for instance, material that can be quickly erased and re-used) or they can be in electronic forms. Even the raw materials for print media could be held fairly close to the possibilities of neighborhood self-sufficiency and responsibility. The point is not that a neighborhood would thus close itself off from all other communications. The point is simply that the neighborhood can have internal communications sufficient to a fully developed politics of internal freedom and could thereafter enjoy any extended communications with a world of other communities that might be desired.

Computers, of course, have made the storage and retrieval of information a matter of the most drastically reduced scale. They are adaptable also to local manufacture. They are perfectly suited to neighborhood use. Used in neighborhoods, with local familiarity and control, the computer might be seen as more of a tool than a weapon.

Even the problem of traditional information, exemplified in the library, is solvable in a way most compatible with neighborhood scale. Microfiche readers of great sophistication, but happily of reasonably straightforward and small-scale manufacturing technique, mean that the entire contents of the Library of Congress can be stored in a small office space, taking up no more room than the pet food section of a supermarket.

Since the material base of local liberty, and particularly the local liberty of city neighborhoods, requires attention to the material world, it necessarily involves science and technology. The potential for local liberty of rural neighborhoods is scarcely arguable or, as a matter of fact, often disputed.

Fortunately, most neighborhoods already have many citizens within them who represent a scientific turn of mind and who are familiar with various technologies. Again, it is from the realm of opinion, and not the realm of material good sense, that we have derived the notion that neighborhood "skills" must be administrative skills rather than material skills. Material skills have for so long been accepted as merely the purchased property of corporations and the state that seeing them as the ordinary skills of ordinary people in ordinary settings may seem novel or even unsettling.

But the fact is that there are craftspeople, technicians, and people with general scientific training in most neighborhoods. A tool and skill inventory of an urban neighborhood would be revealing and encouraging. Local schools, of course, have science and shop teachers. The entire life of the neighborhood is riddled with skills—putting things back together, plugging them in, and so forth.

Also, it would scarcely seem reasonable to say that pursuit of actual scientific knowledge (which at root involves what Albert Einstein called "common sense carried to an extreme") should be beyond neighborhood people. If science is beyond them, or us, what can be in our grasp? Only opinion? Only singing and dancing? At any rate, in discussing the material base of local liberty, it would seem foolish to assume that scientific knowledge is impossible to people simply because of where they live! When a neighborhood is a university, nobody is surprised that there are people in the neighborhood who understand plasma physics. Ten blocks away there need be no more surprise if anyone *wants* to understand plasma physics there. The problem is not that brains change when they go across town but only that opportunities change. And, in a neighborhood aware that much of its liberty depends upon prudential relationships to the material and natural world, and understanding also that this relationship is mediated through scientific knowledge as well as political decision, it should be no great trick for people *to acquire* the knowledge necessary to their civic needs.

In summary: The material base for local liberty exists. The decision to have or not have local liberty is just that, a decision, a decision derived from human will. Nature does not abhor liberty. It is rather neutral on the subject, chaining most life forms to a totalitarianism of instinct and reflex that makes liberty extraneous. Humans, however, have choices. Humans speculate and analyze and deliberately change environments. Humans make choices between those changes. And one choice in nature is local liberty.

Adams-Morgan is a small country afloat in a great city. It is a neighborhood of some seventy blocks in the center—almost the exact center—of Washington, D.C. The population is 58 percent black, 22 percent Latin American, 18 percent white, with the remainder mostly Middle Eastern. It is a neighborhood in transition; as a small country, it's in decline.

For a while, during a rash and wonderful tilt at making itself a truly participatory community, Adams-Morgan was a fascinating culture in which to live. More recently it has become a prime target for speculative selling and buying, a bullish market well beyond the means of the people who first made it a good neighborhood. Its nature is slowly changing to chic—from workshops to boutiques, from bars to cocktail lounges, from a heady whirl with community government to the island life of townhouses with barred windows and residents whose concerns are global, where, for a time, they were local. If all goes as it now is going, soon it will not even be a neighborhood, much less a small country. Adams-Morgan will be just another place in Washington. An address. A fancy one.

For almost five years, Therese Machotka and I lived together and worked with hundreds of people in the neighborhood striving for an entirely different future. Some are still at it. We quit several years ago and moved to West Virginia. What happened—and continues to happen—goes something like this.

I spent my childhood in the neighborhood, got my first haircut in a barber shop there that is now a locksmith's shop, kissed my first girl in the part of Rock Creek Park that borders Adams-Morgan. I had my first fistfight under the bridge that carries fashionable Connecticut Avenue safely past the northwest edge of the neighborhood and went to one of the two schools from which Adams-Morgan derives its name.

After forty years or so I came back. What had been comfortably middle class had become very lower class, a shambles about to become a slum. But it was cheap—and it tolerated hippies both socially and economically. This was the mid-1960s. The hippies who moved in were mostly stoned, mostly exiles, mostly useless; and the neighborhood slipped down another notch. Venereal disease went up. Panhandling became the local growth industry, and welfare blacks and zonked-out whites began to drink Ripple together and curse the dark night of colonialism, oppression, and shortages of good hash and sturdy H.

By the late 1960s something began to stir in the debris. In the fashion of the opening scene in *2001*, some stoned-out hippie got sick of the faucet dripping or the VW van not running—some minor calamity—and, wonder of wonders, got straight long enough to *fix it*. Perhaps the change began more subtly, perhaps it was more complex, or, at least, perhaps some social jargonist could describe it that way. My own experience was that it was fairly simple and direct. Somebody had to do something. Someone did. It worked. And the world changed a little. Odd jobs became a substitute for panhandling, and proved more productive. How-to books began sliding self-consciously onto shelves alongside the great mystics and the red-hot revolutionaries. And something very important indeed began to happen to the residential warrens in which the stoned citizens had compartmented themselves. They turned into working communes, group residences with shared chores, aspirations, shared values, and, very often, shared work.

By the end of the 1960s there were probably sixty to

seventy-five functioning communes in the neighborhood, and a burst of productive energy emanated from them. A worker-managed grocery store opened and became an immediate success, a place to shop with good prices and a good-natured persistence in nutritional education. Then a second one opened. A newspaper popped up in the neighborhood, about the neighborhood. Then a second one. A record store. Several bookstores. Craftspeople, from potters to auto mechanics, began hawking their wares from community billboards, tree posters, street corners. Musicians rented a storefront and began nightly improvisational sessions—jazz, rock, country, classical. Several graphic arts shops opened. A community credit union was started. And, perhaps most important, a community government proclaimed itself, called a meeting, and actually got off the ground.

The community government rose, like everything else, from the rubble of failures immediately past. Heretofore Adams-Morgan, neighborhood organizations, and civic associations had simply sought to present resolutions *to* the city government. None had dared the idea of *being* a government.

At the first meeting to discuss something new, it was young white products of the counterculture and the New Left (but mainly the counterculture) who made the breakthrough. Rather than simply have another neighborhood organization, why not go a step further? The step was toward a town meeting. The idea was remarkably nonideological, considering that some of the proponents were burning inside with visions of storming the Winter Palace, of looking like Lenin, of smashing the oppressors, of this and of that. A town meeting, it was argued in practical terms and, fortunately, in purely homely language, would provide a forum in which people in the neighborhood could get together, discuss their problems, discuss solutions, and then actually decide what they themselves could do. This instead of just complaining to a massively sluggish city bureaucracy.

The thing wasn't even called a town meeting. It was called

the "Adams-Morgan Organization," AMO. At its first meeting someone said that the streets were dirty. Someone else suggested that we all get together and have a clean-up day. The meeting agreed. Signs were mimeographed on a church duplicator, paper donated by a neighborhood resident with a job in a print shop. The neighborhood was saturated with the information that AMO members (then only about 300) were going to sweep down the neighborhood's main street over the weekend.

About 200 people actually got out and swept. Probably almost all of the neighborhood's 40,000 total population at least heard about it. AMO's membership, based on a growing belief that it would be a doing and not just a talking organization, began to grow. By the time we left, it had passed 3000.

The town meetings, or "AMO Assemblies" as they were actually called, were the most exciting political experiences I have ever had. After tasting a participatory democracy, I would never want to trade it for a merely representative one.

A small problem: Most of the participants in the assembly never thought they had *left* a representative democracy. The idea of participation versus representation did not jell for everyone.

There was an obvious cultural dimension to the problem. The counterculture people were actually looking for a new way to make social decisions and, specifically, a way to do it without social exploitation of one group by another. The idea of a town meeting—with people who make decisions being responsible also for carrying them out, and not merely for getting someone else to do it—was understandable and inspiring to them. One consequence was the counterculture types made up at least half of every meeting.

Blacks in the neighborhood had a clearly different view. The rhetoric of participation was accepted and so was the form. But the reality behind it was not participation at all. It was power. Blacks, at least in that neighborhood and at that time, were not interested in changing the way social decisions

41

were made. What they wanted was to have the power to make those decisions—to have power *in,* not power *to change,* the system. Whites who do not understand this can make fearsome mistakes in assessing the meaning of black-white alliances for social change.

There was just as deep a cultural bias to the work that was of prime interest to Therese and to me. We were among the most active participants in the town meeting, to be sure, but the work that actually preoccupied us had to do with science and technology. Not science and technology in the abstract or globally or grandly. Science and technology to fit Adams-Morgan precisely.

The interest derived from a scholarly project at the Institute for Policy Studies, with whose work Therese and I had been associated. One IPS project was to study and catalogue ways of life and social agreements in which citizens were full participants and not just voters at best and colonized subjects at worst.

Because the politics which Therese and I share emphasizes decentralization, our work at IPS was directed toward seeing the extent to which science, as a thinking process, and technology, as techniques and tools, could be made part of and directly support everyday life.

Our unifying proposition was this: If there was to be a free society, one in which people could be responsible for their actions, be cooperative individuals rather than coerced corporate parts, there would have to be a supporting material base. Freedom cannot float in the air as mere theory. It must rest on solid earthy ground. The material base, we felt, would have to be one in which people generally could develop, deploy, and maintain the tools of everyday life and production, directing them democratically rather than being directed by them. Such a relationship to science and technology would have to have relevance to a neighborhood. Our neighborhood was Adams-Morgan.

Our first step was just to meet and talk on a regular basis

42

with others who shared some part of our notion. We did it weekly, at first with a half dozen people, a couple of engineers we had met through the peace movement, some craft friends, and students. Others soon joined and soon tired of talking. Therese and I were able to coax a neighborhood clinic operated by Children's Hospital into letting us have unused space in the warehouse building they rented. Therese agreed to put most of her salary as an editor into buying equipment and paying stipends for work. Our talk group became a project that we called "Community Technology."

Our weekly meetings continued, sometimes crowded with forty or fifty visitors, as an information-sharing process. A young physicist with superb general mechanical skills came on full-time for a subsistence share of the money Therese made available. (I just covered our living expenses by writing, welding, selling metal sculpture, and occasionally lecturing.) Our experiments began.

Food, it seemed to us, was the place to start. What could be more basic? Also, the idea of developing, deploying, and maintaining a technology of food production in the middle of a city, and in a ghetto neighborhood at that, seemed as stern a test of our general propositions as could be imagined. The whole idea flew right in the face of conventional wisdom.

First there was the land problem. There's no land for growing food in a city. If there is any open space, it's too much trouble. If you want to be a farmer, go to the country. The arguments that outside critics launched against our project were certainly varied. Neighbors on the other hand often took the attitude that the idea was sort of crazy but what the hell. One of our first mistakes probably took hold right there. We began to confuse toleration of our work with actual support for it.

The land problem was easily solved. Food grows not in an abstraction called "land" but in a reality called "someplace nutritious to put down roots." Space for this reality need be only that—space. We located a lot of it. First the rooftops. The neighborhood is one of houses, typically three-story row houses. The roofs are almost all flat. So are the roofs of the apartment houses. On very strong roofs, organic soil can be spread, or boxed, for growing vegetables. Therese and I grew such a garden. Less sturdy roofs could accommodate the lighter demands of hydroponic growing—cultivating plants in tanks of liquid nutrients or in light sand, the nutrients seeping through it. Friends who began a companion enterprise, the Institute for Local Self-Reliance, a still growing and prospering activity, operated a hydroponic garden with storybook success and wildly bountiful crops. They also managed to fill virtually the entire neighborhood's demand for bean sprouts from a single basement facility.

More traditionally, we worked with kids in the neighborhood to establish regular gardens in vacant lots and in any back-yard space that people wanted to make available. The entire back lot of our warehouse was covered with dirt that we begged from local excavators, and it became a community garden. Also, using the vegetable wastes from several local grocery stores, leaves from suburban lawns, and horse manure from a park police stable, we maintained about ninety feet of compost pits behind the warehouse.

To supplement the vegetable crop we looked around for a suitable meat animal. Cows were out. Too big. Rabbits didn't make it. Too cuddly. Chickens wouldn't do. Too noisy. How about fish?

One of our group, an organic chemist, was experienced in trout farming and suggested that we work up some high-density indoor tanks for raising that fancy fish.

Jeffrey Woodside, our resident physicist and jack-of-all-trades; his immensely energetic friend Esther Siegal; our chemist, Fern Wood Mitchell; and Therese built tanks of fiberglass-covered plywood, arranged water recirculation with pumps from discarded washing machines, and contrived filters for the fish waste made of boxes filled with calcite chips (the standard marble chips sold in garden supply stores) into which a few cups of ordinary vacant-lot soil had been poured to provide a bumptious strain of nitrifying bacteria to feed on the ammonia in the fish waste.

The bacteria kept the water clean, the pumps and some well-placed baffles kept the tank water moving in a strong current, the fish (which we first reared from eggs in ordinary aquarium tanks) swam strongly, ate heartily of the commercial feed that we first used as a convenience, and grew as fast as fish in streams. Surprisingly to us, the rate at which they converted their feed to flesh was better than one ounce of fish for each two ounces of food, about 500 percent more efficient than beef cattle, and as good as that champion barnyard converter, the chicken. Our installation, neatly tailored to urban basements, produced five pounds of fish per cubic foot of water. A typical basement in the neighborhood could produce about three tons annually at costs substantially below grocery store prices.

A young stonemason in the group began experimenting with small completely self-contained bacteriological toilets and had fair success suggesting that any neighborhood could unhook itself from conventional sewer systems and their inefficiency and pollution.

A marine engineer in the group, lately turned solar experimenter, built a very effective solar cooker that tracked the sun automatically, cost under $300 to build, and provided up to 400 degrees F. of cooking heat on an indoor hotplate from energy collected by an outside mirror in the shape of a three-foot-long trough.

An elementary school science teacher built a solar collector out of catfood cans that heated household air to about 120 degrees F.

The group generally began discussing the design of a shopping cart that could be built in the neighborhood; a self-powered platform that would handle most of the neighborhood's heavy moving chores; a neighborhood chemical factory to make household cleaners, disinfectants, insecticides, and aspirin; and a neighborhood methanol plant to take local garbage and turn it into a portable fuel with properties roughly similar to gasoline.

We sought a grant from the National Science Foundation to start a neighborhood science center in which people of the neighborhood could work toward understanding the natural science of the neighborhood itself, of the tool and technique possibilities, and of the appropriate role of science and technology in the community. The NSF sent a sociologist out to look us over and turned our application down cold. We did not meet the government-approved definition of a neighborhood self-help program. Even at NSF such programs are aimed at enhancing the ability of neighborhood people not to produce their own wealth and future but to better obtain welfare assistance.

Government programs aim at getting money for poor people. Our hope was that knowledge would in the long run be more useful, provide more money, and eventually strike at the system-causes of poverty. Government believes that poverty is just a lack of money. We felt, and continue to feel, that poverty is actually a lack of skill, and a lack of the self-esteem that comes with being able to take some part of one's life into one's own hands and work with others toward shared—call them social—goals.

It will not be denied that ours was and remains a middle-class attitude, quite classical and thoroughly Western. It stands opposed to the elitist notion of mandarins caring for benighted peasantry, an attitude that prevails today in various modern trappings, among them enlightened capitalism, state socialism, and welfare statism.

But so much for the big notions and nations.

It seems these same lines get drawn in the participatory neighborhood. At assembly meetings, reports of our work were always greeted with applause and great enthusiasm. We were a showcase bunch of wizards doing wonderful far-out things. Our appeals for neighbors to join us in the work—to help build, expand, improve the fish farm; to move the gardens along; to experiment with new ways of growing; to start stores and even factories based on our skills and tools—got choruses of "right ons"—and no participants.

Instead, the heavy work of the assembly began to emphasize direct appeals to government agencies and foundations for grants; there were complaints about landlord abuses instead of plans to buy them out.

Meeting after meeting, for instance, the idea of pooling money was brought up, pooling money to establish neighborhood ownership of key properties, to provide homes for the evicted, to set new patterns of ownership for a new kind of neighborhood. Plenty of "right ons." No cash. Was there any cash? Of course. Even people on welfare have disposable incomes. The pool of money needed to buy our neighborhood would have been relatively modest, the weekly equivalent of a carton of cigarettes or a bottle of whiskey from each member of the assembly. Of course, it would have meant sacrifice. Some of us have little enough pleasure, and a smoke or a drink is to be treasured beyond all the promises of paradise.

There were, in fact, jobs aplenty in the neighborhood. The District government, sternly charged by federal authorities with making the streets safe for visiting dignitaries, including congressmen and bureaucrats, had decided that bribery was the best tool available for getting young people off the streets. The District funded programs through which teenagers could draw a minimum of $1.75 an hour for the exertion of signing in in the morning and signing out in the afternoon. There is no convincing evidence that this did anything to halt incipient criminality. It seemed to me that it accomplished a great deal more in terms of separating young people from the possibilities of self-reliance. It anchored them more firmly to habitual dependence on unearned incomes and thus on the people who dispense them—be they the wielders of welfare programs or those less-willing providers, the victims of larceny.

A question began nagging during a lot of our work and

discussion: Was our vision of neighborhood self-help crumbling along racial lines? Are blacks particularly disabled when it comes to seeking alternatives to welfare programs?

The Adams-Morgan neighborhood, like Washington overall, is certainly black. The people who seemed to talk most about and do the least in support of our group's proposals were black. Young whites seemed to respond more to skill- and production-centered activities. Those are solidly middle-class values out of a primarily European culture. Blacks have been the victims, rather than the beneficiaries, of both the values and the culture.

Blacks think black, as they continually say. So black has come to mean poor and oppressed. Black demands have come to mean black reparations: to be given something rather than seeking the chance to do something.

Everyone in our largely white group deeply sympathized with the fact of oppression. Some went further and supported the implicit strategy for social redress through reparation rather than community renewal.

My problems and doubts began with my conclusion (shared in large measure by Therese) that such a strategy was not only useless, it was unjust, crippling, and ethically debilitating.

While nursing such doubts, the Community Technology work began to seem quite different to me than it had at the beginning. First, it did not seem to have any real relevance to what was happening in the neighborhood. The hope that people would want to fashion new lives based upon new knowledge and new skills seemed now very romantic and very wrong. Desirable still, but at present hopeless.

There was another problem: crime. It too fell along racial lines.

At one AMO meeting a young white man reported a particularly vicious hold-up, beating, and rape that had occurred at a communal house. Before any discussion could get under way, he was asked the color of the victims. White. He was asked the color of the attackers. Black. With blacks in the

48

majority, that particular meeting simply moved on to another topic. Not another word of discussion was possible.

This typified a particularly destructive, if fashionable, impulse among both blacks and whites to dismiss all discussion of crime as oppressively racist, despite the fact that blacks are the principal victims of black crime.

Another major victim of unchecked, because unmentionable, crime was the AMO group itself. Keeping a typewriter available in the office was always a rigorous exercise in security, and none too successful at that. Money needed for a variety of things was eaten up simply replacing ordinary equipment rather than attacking the roots of the problem with the same energy so effectively mustered for battles with landlords and sanitation and welfare services.

An inevitable result of an undiscussed rising crime situation was the deterioration of the neighborhood and the easing of entry for the next wave of residents, the ones who could afford better security and who did not mind living in a small fortress so long as the address was fashionable. It happened in Adams-Morgan.

But could neighborhood people have coped with crime? I certainly think so. It would mean first coping with their own children, facing them down, creating families that would absorb their energies and deserve their loyalties. Not easy. Not likely. And particularly not likely when parents are opiated by a welfare existence, and where schools are simply disciplinarian baby sitters, offering young people no creative alternative to violence as the way to get out, to get up, to get even.

It was the growing crime and violence that finally ended our residence in the neighborhood. After being robbed on the average of once every sixty days or so, Therese, for one, felt terror at night in the neighborhood. We both resented the continuing loss of things, particularly since our income was roughly at the poverty level; but, being larger and a male, I had not felt the terror. After a time, Therese felt it sharply enough to leave. We moved to West Virginia. Having been raised in rural Wisconsin, Therese found these hills immediately hospitable in ways the city's streets had never been. I still love the city neighborhood but have also experienced a sort of homecoming in these hills richer than I ever could have anticipated.

The neighborhood is still there, of course. So also are every one of the problems that we should have addressed more squarely during our time with Community Technology. Or perhaps, from this new distance, I only see them differently.

I do believe from my experience in the small workings of Community Technology that even science can live in a neighborhood. Ordinary people can get together to discuss physical principles just as well as they can get together to discuss abstruse political principles in the fashion of young radicals and young conservatives.

But the entire relationship of our work to the neighborhood suggests something else in the short run: that the culture of poverty is not easily diverted beyond itself. In that culture, immediate relief in terms of program handouts is the "cure" too commonly prescribed. It cannot easily be changed. It was not changed in Adams-Morgan over a period of years despite some most adventurous experiments by highly charged people. The culture of poverty will run its course. How long that course is, I have no idea. I am convinced, however, that if the culture of poverty is to be broken in any black neighborhood it will be broken by black people, not by starry-eyed whites talking soul patter.

Coming from his Chicago base, Jesse Jackson lectured black Washington teenagers on the need to learn skills rather than gripe endlessly about feeling oppressed. He was virtually run out of town for his effort. Still powerfully at large in the city is the attitude of a former superintendent of schools, Barbara Sizemore, a vigorous opponent of Jackson. To her, the entire problem is power, black versus white. She is less interested in a freer or better world than in a black one. I recall her once being quoted as advocating that black children should not

50

even study white subjects. And what are white subjects? Mathematics and science. What should black children study? Those things that come naturally—singing and dancing, perhaps. It sounds to me like an old and foul joke.

The assembly, meantime, shows signs of attrition as the old idea of representation begins to recover the ground lost to the experiment in community participation. The assembly has become more a bandstand for aspiring politicians than a forum for people. To still dream of something entirely different requires the understanding that this kind of subversion is likely to happen time and time again.

While the assembly was occupied mainly with local problem solving, and before conventional constituency politics overcame it, it was greatly effective. People who had been shy spoke out. People who had seemed without hope sparked to new life.

Meantime, a similar and sad malady has affected some of the worker-managed enterprises that brought the neighborhood to life in the first place. The malady is ideology. For several years the workers in the enterprises toiled hard and long at being useful to the neighborhood and good friends to each other. Now several of the key groups have begun to work equally hard at becoming friends not of people but of history. They spend hours behind closed doors thrashing out the correct line on this or that remote political issue or revolutionary posture. Previously, in open meetings, they drew in—and on—the neighborhood. They have forfeited once-real social power in Adams-Morgan to become no more than images of history floating in the clouds of rhetoric and pure theory.

Blacks by and large have moved wholly into the rat race of conventional politics and foundation grantsmanship. And upper-middle-class *arrivistes*, both black and white, share no concern for the neighborhood beyond the recent trendiness of its address.

Some of the original spirit persists, however. The people at the Institute for Local Self-Reliance continue to do what they

51

can, but more frequently this entails reaching into other communities. With Therese gone and rent no longer provided, our Community Technology warehouse has been turned very usefully into a soap factory, operated by Jeff and Esther, stalwarts of our group from the start. They make a living at it and they try to teach a few kids in the neighborhood how to read. They grin and bear the annual vandalism of the gardens by kids who think that vegetables are underclass food—TV snacks, beer, and dope being the fare of real operators.

The weekly meetings have ended. Information is swapped by phone and mail these days. But almost everyone who was involved in the effort retains faith that it was a right thing to do and that someday the memory of it will be an inspiration to the neighborhood that finally does decide to take its culture, its lives, and its productive possibilities wholly into its own hands. Such a neighborhood will not change the world overnight as in the fervid dreams of the young revolutionaries. But it will change part of the world, possibly the part of the world that you live in.

A vision of what it could be like.

Exactly ten years after the District's first home-rule primary election, it will be 1984, the date famed for predictions of the ultimate rule of Big Brother.

In a Washington and an America following a path of centralized power over an expanded bureaucracy, the 1984 elections here could be merely a ritual support of a puppet city government—a little brother for the Big Brother ruler.

But the signs are *not* all pointing that way. Indeed, heady new whiffs of freedom seem to be sensed everywhere. By 1984, Washington, free and bountiful, could be a dream, not a nightmare, come true. If so, a chronicler of the time might reflect on the decade in this way:

It came as no particular surprise to anyone that the first of the great changes came in the Adams-Morgan section, that mixed seventy-block bag of artists, craftspeople, businesspeople, antibusinesspeople, bureaucrats, cooperators, radicals, conservatives, welfare families, workers of all kinds, loafers, hucksters, hypsters, and hipsters.

Shortly after the first mayoral election, as a matter of fact, during a neighborhood street fair, the fairgoers by obvious conspiratorial arrangement simply tore up the entire street, blocked it at both ends, and began preparing the ground for planting. In the spring the first flowers appeared. By the end of the summer the entire neighborhood was not only using the street as a park but was supplying a significant part of its nutrition from the gardens which checkerboarded the street. Automobiles, in the meantime, parked very handily in angle-in lines at each end of the street.

The city, of course, had virtual fits about the citizen action in converting the street to a park. But, in the jockeying for power and politicking that marked the transition to home rule there were more situations in which the citizens could, literally, stand off the government while experimenting with their new-found freedom. And, in cases like the spontaneous park, the effects were so practical and popular that the forces of status quo looked silly anyway.

There was also the very important development in Anacostia, where the people, totally neglected for so long by so many politicians, decided to make a new kind of politics just for their own benefit. Moving from the base of their neighborhood advisory council, they instituted a town meeting of the entire neighborhood. When that appeared too cumbersome for such a large area, they sensibly divided into six parts and instituted six separate town meetings that met monthly and one federated meeting that met twice a year to discuss problems relative to all the neighborhoods.

One important effect was that people got a hold on their own civic lives. Those who had cynically stayed away from any civic activities for years found that airing their gripes and making their suggestions at town meetings, and seeing actions get under way through citizen participation rather than downtown red tape, made their entire lives take on new meaning, new excitement, and a new sense of dignified purpose. Unlike any other form of political activity they had ever seen, the town meeting was democracy in action. Things got done because *they* did it.

It was the matter of work, as a matter of fact, that moved the Anacostia town meeting toward one of the most significant of all the changes in the burst of freedom and creativity that eventually turned Washington into what some people called "New Athens" and others called "that crazy place."

The question of neighborhood use of an abandoned garage–repair space came up for discussion. First suggestions followed old familiar patterns. The space would be good for teenage dances. It might be used for a community office. Someone suggested it might be used as a soup kitchen for the unemployed. That seemed to spark it. Why not use it to attack the problem of unemployment itself? someone asked. Why couldn't the community acquire the space, which was tax delinquent, for a business of its own? After a few hours of discussion there seemed to be agreement that, rather than an ordinary business, the space should be used for some sort of labor-intensive light manufacturing process.

Anacostia's booming community bicycle factory, whose products are now seen all over town, was the result. It was the first of the many actual production facilities, managed by the workers and owned by the community, that helped turn Washington from a federal dependent, with red tape as its most important product, into a self-reliant and vigorous place with an economy of its own.

The Georgetown Furniture and Cabinet Guild, of course, followed very quickly, using a warehouse space which had previously been seen only as useful in housing fashionable peddlers of bric-a-brac to the rich. By working as a cooperative venture, and by trying to be part of the city's new economic life at a community level rather than standing apart and just chasing profits, the guild introduced furniture designs that were not only of incredibly good quality but available at prices that eventually drove most of the junk furniture out of stores where working people had for years been sadly exploited and overcharged.

The basement transistor "factories" near Howard University and a warehouse-sized fabric mill in the same area made a nationally significant point about the utility of small-scale production which had been slighted for so long simply because people viewed production as only an economic activity, not a social one. Everyone associated with the new burst of activity agreed that the effect on the neighborhoods and on the people was every bit as significant as the sheer dollars generated.

By the fifth Year of Freedom, as the years quickly came to be known and numbered, the relationship of these production centers to the entire life of the city was clear. That year the first Columbia Electric Car rolled out of a neighborhood factory instituted in space formerly used for city government storage in the Northeast section beyond Catholic University. By then the number of town meetings—which had become the characteristic form of local organization, reducing the power of the central government to that of virtual storekeeping and ceremony—had risen to more than 200, giving forms of direct participation unequaled in any city. The Columbia Car has proven, as is now well known, a fine service vehicle throughout the city, more than making up for the banning of conventional vehicles on all but a few through arterial streets.

This year, of course, with the introduction of the so-called Gallaudet Gasser, the hydrogen-fueled car designed by a communal house of engineers living in the Gallaudet College area, the entire subject will come in for new debate and decision as the neighborhoods have a new technology to consider.

Perhaps nowhere more than in the Well Body Health Center at what once was St. Elizabeths Hospital, is the effect of town meetings more clear. The facilities at St. Elizabeths, used for so-called mental cases for so many years, became available for other purposes after another of the town meeting decisions. Considering the amount of money allocated under traditional systems for mental hospitals, and also considering the dubious nature of treatment in them, the neighborhoods decided on an experimental scattering of the patients throughout the neighborhoods, in what amounted to therapeutic foster homes, with the money formerly used for the centralized treatment now allocated for special and specific needs, such as the special cases involving live-in attendants to stay with the supposedly violent.

Absorbed into neighborhoods where they could slowly become a part of everyday life rather than constant clinical subjects, the former patients in almost every case improved and became able to live peaceful lives, with self-respect and in many cases with opportunities to use skills and talents that their clinical experiences had ignored and suppressed.

St. Elizabeths, emptied by the successful experiment, became available for another one, every bit as striking. It became an intercommunity health learning center. (The name Well Body Health Center was the contribution of a ten-year-old girl who wandered in one day and casually suggested that half the kids in her school class would be willing to spend a summer working at the center if they could use the swimming pool every day.)

The idea was to have a health (not sickness) facility in which people with health problems, or the desire to avoid them, plus medically skilled people, plus people regarded in the past as "only" maintenance people, could work together in a learning and doing center.

By that time also, virtually every neighborhood had made some sort of local health advance as well. The Chevy Chase Community Clinic, in the neighborhood's long-standing community center, was one of the first. It began, as old-timers there now recall, as pretty much a substitute for the old-fashioned community drugstore where the pharmacist on duty was a sort of one-man medical band, extracting a splinter one minute, getting a cinder out of the eye next, advising on a cough medicine, talking about diet, and so forth—a sort of paramedic way before the term became fashionable. At any rate, at the Chevy Chase facility, a few young people trained in paramedic skills got together to form an after-work facility that would attempt to deal with the many health problems that, while not requiring a fully trained doctor, seemed to make up a substantial part of the pressure that had made obtaining health care in Washington as difficult as in any other city.

A significant extension of the idea followed in at least three other neighborhoods almost immediately, when people there decided to have their own drugstores, combining the paramedic services of the earlier facility with actual prescription and other services. Such facilities, the town meetings in those areas argued, are far more than just commercial enterprises, so closely do they affect the lives of the citizens, and therefore should be operated with the fullest citizen participation.

Even before the end of colonial status, several of the city's neighborhoods had developed a commercial life that was quite appropriate to the turn things took during the early Liberty years. Worker-managed stores such as Fields of Plenty, Stone Soup, and Bread and Roses were both a joy for shoppers and proof that worker management worked internally, while community involvement in general commercial decision making worked socially. Second-generation efforts such as the South Capitol Street Hardware, Science, and Tool Store broadened the concept into areas that supported very appropriately the wave of do-it-yourself parks, street benches, kiosks, playgrounds, and housing renovations that became as familiar in Washington as step scrubbing had been in Baltimore a couple of generations earlier.

The development of the idea of community apprenticeships for schoolchildren by several of the neighborhood schools also enriched the movement.

Of all the ideas of community cooperation on projects that had formerly been the exclusive province of well-heeled outsiders, there probably was none that aroused more immediate and citywide interest than the Columbia Eagles, the city's community-owned, player-managed big-league baseball club. When the club won the pennant in Freedom Year Eight, the result was a civic celebration which lasted a full week. There were festivals, carnivals, and an epic round-the-clock concert that alternated the Columbia Symphony, the community follow-on from the old National Symphony, with Morales, the great Mount Pleasant Latin rock band. The by now carless downtown area was made to order for the occasion.

At the very outset of the Washington renaissance, a group of students and faculty at Washington Technical Institute turned

Washington's waste (once the full-time odorous chore of Blue Plains) from a problem into a resource.

The first phase was the complete reorientation of the trash collection system. Several neighborhoods, despairing of the cumbersome, careless manner in which trash had been collected or neglected under the city government proper, had already demanded and received the right to handle it in their own way, retaining an appropriate share of tax revenue for the purpose.

One neighborhood had actually turned the collection system into an asset from which certain social services were financed, by getting the community to agree to stashing trash in "category" containers (garbage in one, solid materials in another), which made possible a profitable salvage operation. Another neighborhood set up its collection operation as a cooperative, with neighborhood people taking turns, as a sort of social "tax," doing work which, they agree, is better shared than dumped on one or two people full time.

Several other neighborhoods, pooling resources, found that a collection system using pedal carts that ferried the trash quickly and quietly to regular trucks on the edge of the neighborhood worked well economically.

It was with the change of the human-waste system, however, that the WTI students became involved. Their proposition was to try to close up, in effect, the entire sewage-waste system, using it as a neighborhood resource rather than letting it grow wildly as a citywide problem. A six-block area near Fort Slocum Park was the first full-scale experiment. In it, the entire sanitary sewage system was diverted at a convenient main to a waste-use facility set up in a remodeled one-family house. In the house, waste entered large digesting chambers where, odorlessly and without any atmospheric or other pollution, the wastes were broken down into usable methane gas and very nutritive organic fertilizer, whose sale also helped finance community services, while the methane was recycled into the neighborhood as an almost complete substitute for

59

commercial cooking gas. (In one neighborhood using a version of the same system, it has been reported that all of the local cooking energy is supplied from waste-generated gas.)

In Spring Valley, a variation on the same theme—but more appropriate to the large, rather isolated housing there—was arrived at during the same period. Individual houses, it was discovered, could disconnect from the sanitary sewage system altogether by installing small-scale versions of the waste digesters, providing a substantial supplement to cooking gas and enough organic fertilizers to make the local lawns bloom greener than ever before.

Within three years it was apparent that the entire citywide sanitary system could be abandoned. The final step was a larger but still local digester plant, which was installed in the first six floors of a downtown office building.

The fact that this year both the Anacostia and the Potomac were open for swimming attests to the plant's success.

But it was at the other end of the problem, the eating end, that some of the most innovative work was done in the earliest years. Glover Park led the way in one of the two most important developments. First, there was the W Street Fish Factory. Thanks to innovative work done by local technologists and scientists, who took the idea of neighborhood self-sufficiency as requiring a material as well as a socio-political base, a way was discovered to raise high quality fish (mainly rainbow trout and the delicious Asian Tilapia) in extremely concentrated but absolutely healthy conditions. The earliest experiment, on Fulton Street, grew five tons of fish in the basement of an ordinary single-family dwelling. By the time the W Street neighborhood set up its cooperative factory in a surplus geodesic dome on the edge of Glover-Archbold Park (the familiar multicolored landmark that children nowadays are fond of calling the "flying saucer"), the technique was developed so that the entire fish-protein needs of a neighborhood could be filled from a space such as the basement of a school building, or a dozen separate houses, or a separate structure as in Glover Park.

Perhaps the most ingenious variation of the fish-farming technique was a small fish-farming operation on 17th Street N.W., which used as feed for its fish a "ranch" of cockroaches obtained from "brood stock" rousted out in a clean-up campaign and fed exclusively from kitchen wastes made available through the local trash separation service. Efforts of a well-known local lawyer to close down the operation were outwitted during the now legendary Cockroach Conflict in which the 17th Street fish farmers threatened, if stopped, to liberate their entire ranch of roaches in the neighborhood of the famed, and futilely fuming, lawyer. (Lawyers generally seemed to have a mixed time of it during the early days of citydom. The rush to local autonomy and experimentation kept plenty of them busy scrapping with the city officials. But the tendency of neighborhoods, once well established with town meetings, to discuss their affairs, to work out most of their own problems in ad hoc and neighborly ways, took away a lot of other legal work.) With the advent in many neighborhoods of regular neighborhood courts, with open hearings where grievances could be aired and, almost inevitably, where common-sense solutions could be found, it seemed that the idea of local self-reliance had effectively shattered another myth, the myth that law is a field so complicated and separated from everyday life that ordinary people cannot understand it. The attitude of the neighborhood courts seemed to be that if law is that esoteric, it had better be brought down to earth. And they did that.

Down to earth also was the next stage of the food production process that had begun with the fish farms. Versions of the old Victory Gardens flourished all over the city during the first, and every subsequent, summer of Washington's liberation.

The next stage wasn't down to earth at all, however. It was quite up in the air! Now, of course, the sight of greenhouses on rooftops is familiar and has even become, to people portraying the Washington skyline, roughly what the skyline at the Battery used to be for New York.

Hydroponic gardening on rooftops yielded some astonishing results. To cite just one, the elderly residents of the Roosevelt

Hotel harvested ten tons of tomatoes from their roof the very first time they tried it—raising the plants with liquid nutrients poured through sand beds supporting the roots, and controlling the temperature and humidity so that year-round growing was possible.

People familiar with the greenhouse skyline are familiar also with those other symbols of an alternative technology that have become characteristic of the city and, increasingly, of the world: the solar collector and the wind generator.

The famed Willard Generator, with its brightly painted designs, has dominated the corner of 14th and F Streets since it was erected atop the Community Research Center in the old Willard Hotel. It is now one of the most copied civic art forms in the world. When it was first erected, however, the Potomac Electric Power Company waged a full-scale attack against it, partly on the basis of defacing the downtown visual character! Shortly after PEPCO was "municipalized" by the federated neighborhoods, a full-scale duplicate of the Willard Generator was lovingly erected atop PEPCO headquarters.

The solar collectors, which are also now a commonplace of everyone's life, and which supply fully half of the city's heating requirements during the winter and considerable amounts of energy for cooling during the summer, started springing up like black caps on many older houses and almost all new ones in the early years and particularly after the entire commercial block of 18th Street below Columbia Road installed collectors in staggered rows to prevent shielding one another. Among other things, the bursting brilliance of the sun glistening onto and off of the collectors turned the street into a daytime display that made the old-fashioned use of spotlights to get attention seem feeble indeed.

For a time there seemed a possibility that the smaller, house-scaled collectors would be abandoned when the vast experimental "sun farm" collector was installed at Soldiers' Home. Its eventual use to supply almost the entire federal power requirements in the Northwest and Northeast areas, however, caused most neighborhoods to stick with plans to keep their alternative energy sources on as local a basis as possible. By now, of course, solar collectors and wind generators are simply a commonplace, although by no means the only alternative sources in the amazingly productive ferment that has grown out of the neighborhoods and out of the city's creative freedom.

When the city achieved its freedom, the Rock Creek Methanol Association was just beginning as the seemingly idiosyncratic effort of a group of businessmen who had become angered by the actions of the petroleum companies during one of the perennial shortages. They began a small-scale methanol plant to see if some measure of self-sufficiency could be achieved right in the middle of the city, knowing that methanol had a long and satisfactory history as a fuel and could be produced, even from some forms of garbage, in small batches and with middling economic feasibility. Although it and some other methanol plants still exist in about seven neighborhoods, the new hydrogen-producing cooperatives—several of them electrolyzing water to produce hydrogen from power generated by wind—are probably more familiar.

It is almost a political cliché now to say that every time a Washington neighborhood came up with one of its screwy ideas a thousand bureaucrats contemplated jumping out their windows—the trend to local self-reliance being the hardest blow ever dealt the federal bureaucracy. That today's federal establishment, concerned mainly with such international technical conventions as the radiation detection service, the Globe Weather Service, and the Maritime Ecology Treaty, is housed largely in the relatively low-lying Pentagon (with the military now pretty much confined to the Polaris System Command at New Britain, Connecticut) is not a tribute to the need to keep bureaucrats out of high-rise buildings so much as it is to the remarkably unanimous action in which the newly liberated city put an absolute ban on future high-rise buildings. Such structures, it will be recalled, gobbled up energy in such indefensible amounts that virtually no one could be found to defend them.

Kennedy Center's conversion soon after that also marked the end of an era. Now familiar and well used as the central facility of the Washington Waterside Park, the center was once a grand ballroom, in effect, for major musical and dramatic events. But, with the emphasis on self-reliance and neighborhood life that followed the decolonization of the city, there was an obvious movement toward decolonizing its artistic life as well. Instead of wanting to be mere spectators at events staged by visiting celebrities, more and more Washingtonians wanted to create and perform themselves. The model of the old Arena Stage and Kreeger Theater became much more appealing than the regal scale of the Kennedy Center and, beginning with the Georgia Avenue Playhouse and the Navy Yard Art Arsenal, neighborhood performing centers sprang up throughout the city to dominate, as they do today, a cultural life which has become, in fact, fully democratized and part of every life rather than a special and separate reflection or mockery of it.

Nowhere is the spreading impact of citywide visual arts involvement more apparent than on the brilliantly decorated sides, tops, fronts, and backs of the city's electric U-Drive cabs, pedicabs, and electric jitney buses. Back when Washington depended upon a fixed state-run surface transportation system of large buses, the most colorful thing about them was their exhaust fumes. Today the average pedicar or electric cab looks like an escapee from an art gallery, thanks in large part to the early Art Co-op artists who traded their designs and decorations in the community for subsistence items.

Looking back on the developments since home rule first became a reality in Washington ten years ago, the only amazing part of the transition is that no one had seemed to be willing to make all these sensible changes way back in 1974, when they had all the technology they needed. Now, it seems so simple.

Utopias are not unattainable; they are simply undesirable. They are undesirable because they mean change and change is the thing most people resist with more determination than any other social action. Any familiar situation is preferred by most of us to any unfamiliar one.

Our very folk language is full of tributes to this fact. The devil you know is better than the devil you don't. I'll stick with what I have. He may be a bastard but he's our bastard. Don't change horses in midstream. A bird in the hand is worth two in the bush. Take the cash and let the credit go, nor heed the rumbling of a distant drum. You go ahead and do it; if it works, I'll join you.

Our own Declaration of Independence gave the notion historic credibility, and also tried to explain why the colonists had waited so long before confronting the Crown: ". . . all Experience hath shewn, that Mankind are more disposed to suffer, while Evils are sufferable, than to right themselves by abolishing the Forms to which they are accustomed."

Utopias are fun to think about, but only the more seriously disaffected or the most idiosyncratic will seriously pursue them, risking or even desiring the changes involved. Christians are particularly strong on this point, making the premature entry into Paradise a serious sin. Suffering what is, rendering Caesar what is his, and so forth are serious Christian virtues. Change is radical. Change is dangerous.

One only has to think about the notorious Utah nerve-gas spill to understand how deeply rooted is this resistance to change. There, after the spill of deadly gas from a training flight, people who were employed by the Army's Chemical Warfare Service, and whose own lives had been endangered by the spill, explained why they did not intend to raise hell about it. In the memorable words of one citizen, who spoke to a friend of mine covering the incident, "We understand it's dangerous, but we need the work." Die-hard (literally) cigarette smokers often say something similar: "I know it'll kill me, but I just can't think about changing now."

You can't teach an old dog new tricks. Right.

Change in the past has seemed to be mostly violent or if not violent so subtle that it hasn't seemed like change at all.

Subtle changes, I believe, have succeeded because they seemed sensible developments rather than changes at all and because they could be accomplished by small groups of people, volitionally, almost as experiments and probably as additions to rather than violent shifts from everyday ways of doing things. The shift from nomadism to agriculture must have been like that, a crop planted experimentally, a success, a season of staying put, then another. And the world changed.

The city, as it developed, did not destroy the towns or villages but simply added a new place to which people could go if they wished.

Trade must have developed sensibly like that too. Some ancient surplus swapped for something else when a visitor chanced by, a sensible hospitality at first, a way to widen possibility afterwards.

Or take that most epochal of inventions, the yoke, dimming even the wheel as the first great technological advance and permitting for the first time the substitution of some other energy for human energy in performing human-directed tasks. Someone did it, others saw it, others did it. It worked. And the world changed again. It was, obviously, not a scary thing.

It is administrative inventions that seem to require violence

66

for success. Priestly and monarchical power have always been pressed on people and borne forward by violence or the threats of it (swords or damnation). Feudalism, capitalism, then state capitalism and state socialism—all have been ridden by violence. The nation-state itself has been aptly described as the institution claiming a monopoly on violence in a given geographical area.

Sometimes, however, it may seem as though what should have been a subtle change becomes a nightmarishly violent one. The spinning machines that ushered in the Industrial Revolution in Great Britain saw not only the Luddite violence of resistance but the broader violence of empire as cotton plantations in distant lands were kept in line by England's immense naval power. But the key there is not the technology, it seems to me. Rather, it is the organizational imperatives of imperial markets and imperial supplies. Had the spinning machines been fed by an emphasis on local British fibers, had they been deployed in village arrays rather than in the administrative fiefdoms of the great families, banks, and politicians—the industrial cities—then the development of the technology would probably have been pacific.

The most notable attribute of any technology has come to be the way in which it is organized and owned, rather than exactly what it does. Gandhi could look at modern machines and see their use in villages. Andrew Carnegie couldn't. Gandhi saw the machines as ways to make things. Carnegie saw them as ways to make fortunes. (Interestingly enough, the American steel industry was quite innovative, quite skillful, and very productive prior to Carnegie and his invention of the heavy industrial trust or monopoly. It wasn't the Bessemer converter that forced the industry into a pattern of big companies that over the years have become scandalously stagnated. It was the administrative invention of industrial growth through merger and acquisition. Steel can be produced by little companies and it can be produced by big companies—both using the same technology. If there is a difference, it would be simply that the smaller companies would be more likely to be inventive, innovative, and vigorously competitive.)

In our time, violent change has seemed the only sort of change. Revolution has been the route of change. Even at this very moment, violence is seen as the great change agent, with terrorism its most contemporary embodiment.

Yet, little has changed except leaders. Standards of living generally have gone up, to be sure. But the general distribution of wealth remains pretty much the same, clumped on the side of the hereditary rich, the predatory politicians, or the violent revolutionary leaders. Generally, in both the capitalist and the socialist world the same modes of production prevail—concentrated ownership, mass markets, mass labor, universalized management. The scale of violence varies, of course. Commissars are more murderous than junior executives. The firing squad is more dramatically lethal than the breadline. Imprisonment is harsher than unemployment. But the modes have been static for so long. Rule is the rule. And even in the United States, the admittedly and happily most free society, the most extolled choices remain the choices among products. And that, alas, is choice trivialized. And it is choice grotesquely trivialized when even politics becomes a matter of choosing among packaged personalities instead of substantive issues.

All is far from lost, however. Because there have been real changes off on the side, almost behind the scenes, changes that make changes possible. Changes that need not be trivial. There have been great changes in knowledge, quantum leaps.

The most revolutionary possibilities in our species' history are the possibilities, here and now, that flow from new knowledge.

Much of the new knowledge is about things, structures, processes. Electronics alone is a revolution of possibilities.

As fond as I am of gadgets, and as crucial as the gadgets are in describing possibility, it is other knowledge that is even more powerful and persuasive. The other knowledge is of life and of ourselves.

There is knowledge enough now to do a much better job, not of conquering nature but of being a decent part of it, of using without ruining it. And there is more knowledge of ourselves, enough to conquer old fears that human beings in the very longest run simply could not be expected to live in peace with themselves, much less the natural world generally.

The fear that human beings are somehow inherently flawed, capable in the long run of little better than armed restraint of a violent, competitive nature, is under illuminating attack all along the fronts of research. From the painstaking archaeological studies by people like the Leakeys comes the warming news that the history of humans is not one of unbroken rampages but rather shows a general disposition to be, wonder of wonders, *civil*, to be attentive to the community of interests represented by those with whom we live as well as to our own ambitions and lusts.

Peter Kropotkin's turn-of-the-century study *Mutual Aid* had turned up similar evidence from the available data on many peoples and places. But Kropotkin, as the most famed anarchist of his time, was felt to be pleading the special case of all libertarians who have seen in the human condition infinite possibility and not only unspeakable peril. The matter-of-fact, reassuringly "scientific" evidence that now supports him is getting a more respectful hearing.

Even in such chilling experiments as the famous one in which people were asked to inflict pain on others (supposedly as part of a very proper clinical test) there is encouraging evidence. Alarmists have made much of the fact that a few people involved in the experiment went so far as to follow orders to inflict the pain even when they believed it would be fatally injurious. Others might take heart from the fact that most of the people involved could not be so cruel and so blindly obedient. They stopped.

And, against the pop-science scare stories of the ethologists who compare human behavior with that of fierce animals in the forest, there are the counterbalancing arguments of scholars such as Ashley Montagu who argue that humans have a distinct personality, are not merely brutes, and as often ascend to the heights as descend to the depths.

There is even that champion scare story of recent years, the discovery of the Ik, an African tribal group so depraved and deprived that they actually make cruelty to one another their most creative activity. First reports of this cruddy bunch darkly suggested that we were peering into the open abyss of our own universal nature—all of us. Since the Ik have not become a continuing obsession, I assume that this dismal first thud of publicity wisely mellowed into realization that what was so astonishing about the Ik has not their universality but their particularity. They are the one and only bunch like that!

And so it goes. So here we are with interesting new knowledge. We can see that human beings are not appallingly bad but are rather a mixed bag, and, most importantly, they are not afflicted with any inescapable tendency to be brutal. For every monstrous psychopath, a bevy of good neighbors. In the personal inventory of most people, the villains may stand out, but the ordinary and decent people outnumber them. And that, of course, is ancient knowledge, newly appreciated.

On top of this we have the new knowledge about the gadgets. First that knowledge tells us that human ingenuity is widely distributed, so widely that it even defies the constraints of formal education and licensing. Edison was an untutored maverick, Einstein a tutored one. One of the finest physicists I know, Ted Taylor, had to be virtually dragged kicking and screaming to get an advanced degree that would permit the "authenticating" of work he had already done! The incredibly promising amorphous semiconductors, which may bring conversion of sunlight to electricity into low-cost availability, have been the scientific specialty of Stanford Ovshinsky, a technological innovator without a college degree.

Our new knowledge of things also tells us that organizational scale is not so important as inspirational and informational intensity.

Most significant new inventions of our time have come from either lone experimenters or small labs, *not* from corporate giants or even government research centers.

Miniaturization has been the most interesting hallmark of the technology most of us think of as the most advanced—electronics. In the technology that may be even more advanced, that of genetic research, there are constant discoveries of the decentralized autonomy of the myriad small organizations that, federated, form our selves. Miniaturization and decentralization abound in the real world. In the administrative world: concentrations of power, consolidation of information, jealous prerogatives; everything is just the reverse of the material world unfolded in technology, and in the humane world unfolded in scholarship.

Item: Acknowledged in the field as the most powerful computer in the entire world, the Cray I is made in a barn on the farm of the designer in Chippewa Falls, Wisconsin. Of course, this is possible because of the relationships and availabilities of parts from many other places—but those places also represent small-scale operations in comparison with the gigantism of the dominating corporations such as General Motors. The largest manufacturer of the silicon chips that have made computers so tiny (and the decentralization of their information processes so possible) has only 8000 employees.

Item: With the cost of photovoltaic cells, used for the direct conversion of sunlight to electricity, falling faster than that of any other power source, there is sense to the notion of individually powering houses, apartments, workplaces, farmsteads, labs, and so forth. The *source* of the energy will be free. Commercial cost of the photovoltaic cells already has dropped to $6000 a peak kilowatt installed, and even though that is a dozen times the cost of conventional power installations, there are at least lab-scale demonstrations which *already* suggest that the cost in the immediate future will drop to $1000 and not too long after to $500 a peak kilowatt. If the pace of the relative costs of photovoltaic cells and conventional power continues (the cells down, the others up), it should not be many years at all before the direct conversion of sunlight to electrical energy—at the point of use!—will be the cheapest form of nonhuman energy available to human beings anywhere on this planet.

It is not Utopian thinking that should make us gasp at this point, it is anti-Utopian thinking. How in the world could anyone in his or her right mind have available information on such a transforming power source as photovoltaic cells and *not* engage in Utopian thinking.

Utopias, given good tools and good neighbors, are in fact the very least we should settle for.

Against Utopia, of course, stands a towering argument that we have heard many times and may hear many times more. The argument, in several parts, runs like this:

People do not want responsibility for their own lives and would rather pass it along to experts who would relieve them of the arduous tasks of making decisions and being socially or politically active when after a hard day's work they just want to relax. Besides, this argument continues, some people are good at one thing, some at another. Leaders are good at leading and should do it. Why should others bother?

The argument has run itself into the ground. The choice is no longer pertinent. The leaders lead on only to new chaos, the experts make grander mistakes. And people generally, coming to realize this, eventually may realize that Utopia is, after all, just a sensible choice.

Which or whose Utopia? The Utopia of those involved, of course. Many different kinds.

That is where the role of the tools may be seen as crucial and where science and technology, operating consciously at the level of the proper locus of Utopia, the locality where people *can* live together in shared respect and on the basis of shared values, can become essential in an everyday sense.

To be able to live at peace, the way people in a community might want to, requires that the material base for that way of

72

living be available. The material base includes tools—even for a community that desires, as some religious ones might, a life of absolute simplicity. The knowledge tools for growing food would at least be a necessity. Additional tools such as greenhousing and hydroponics, depending upon the area, are possibly helpful. The point is that the community to have its freedom must have knowledge of its choices and chances, otherwise it could not be free but would forever be constrained by ignorance of real possibility.

These constraints through ignorance today are far and away the greatest constraints, replacing in their harsh bondages the older constraints of natural resources.

Actually, natural resources never were too harsh a constraint until a growing cosmopolitanism in the world made it appear that those without the resources of the cosmopolitan centers were grievously deprived or, as the phrase became, underdeveloped. Previously, lack of raw materials of one sort had led merely to the development of materials of other sorts. Builders without the bricks of Paris, but with an abundance of bamboo, developed architecture perfectly appropriate to the resource, a truly appropriate technology. And, as a matter of fact, to the extent that a growing and less self-sufficient Paris became dependent for brick on remote suppliers, it became the shackled city, diminished in some freedoms because of outside dependence and yet unable because of commercial imperatives to develop any new, more appropriate technology.

Today's great opportunity is that any community—*any community*—can, with access to knowledge, develop a technology perfectly appropriate to its needs and, moreover, *perfectly appropriate to its resources*. Of course, this means bamboo architecture for some, adobe for others, steel for others—or it means arrangements in free trade to swap back and forth. But, even for swappers a good and solid base seems a sensible first step.

Any community, emphatically, means any community. Communities of the Western world, of course, should be able to see the possibilities as a matter of course. Communities of the so-called Third World, dragooned into so many inappropriate technologies by the cultural forces of their former colonial masters, would also be well served by the concept. In the concept, the communities of a poor nation would first attend to first things: to food, to shelter, and to securing a firm base in basic production before venturing on to foreign trade or to more specialized modes. As things stand, the communities of the Third World are spiraling toward disaster at an unstoppable velocity, facing fearful famines even while former colonial powers erect cheap-labor factories and extractive industries that create rich upper classes, virtually no middle class except for a largely unemployed bunch of liberal arts university graduates, and a tragic lower class. (Recall the 1968–1972 drought and famine in the southwest Sahara area of Africa, where people starved to death even while locally grown food, from irrigated, absentee-owned farms, was being exported to Western Europe by the new entrepreneurs of commercial colonialism.)

Of all communities, however, the ones most likely to be able to take the quickest advantage of making new technologies for their specific purposes would be the very poor inner-city neighborhoods—as previously described but with the addition of the will to *work* at solutions rather than simply ask for them—and medium-sized or small towns nervous about their future, perhaps overdependent on a single or several absentee employers, or on tourism or other "outside" factors for survival.

The small town, for instance, might be tempted to put up a substantial amount of money to create an industrial park to lure industry in. Experience with this technique is mixed. It is costly and it still leaves the town in a dependent position, its future unsecured.

Such a town might well take the next and certainly logical step of owning a small productive industry itself. The experience with the municipal ownership, say, of electrical power

74

generating facilities is so successful that it hardly seems far-fetched that municipal industries would do well. Social ownership is, after all, a familiar activity at the local levels of American life. People who very wisely reject as state socialism the federal ownership of productive facilities have long accepted local social ownership of such things as hospitals (a *very* complex productive or service unit), road repair facilities, agricultural units as in farms associated with county homes, schools, libraries, firefighting companies, even swimming pools and golf courses. To extend that sort of familiar social ownership just a bit to include a productive facility that could help secure the economic future of the entire town seems scarcely romantic but altogether hard-headed and practical.

In taking such a step, a town could draw upon the talents, ad hoc, of craftsmen, technicians, engineers, and others already at work in the town. A most prudent step, well in advance, would be the formation of a town group, committee, or what-have-you to bring such people together regularly to think ahead about the kinds of "tools" for a better community and a more secure future that the town could devise and deploy.

If such a group needed tools to tinker with as they sought out these options, they probably would find them already in place in most towns. Schools have shops and tools. Vocational schools, in particular, have not only equipment but skilled people. Town garages have heavy equipment. Even unused school buses might be an asset in this enterprise, to bring people together for meetings, to take tours of areas that might provide information. Town printing equipment could produce a newsletter to other towns to share information and to inform townspeople of a process in which the participation of all should be welcome.

As a matter of fact, a complete inventory of just how much potentially productive equipment already is owned by any town might be a good first step for citizens concerned with taking their technological future into their own hands.

A group of this sort to which I belong in West Virginia has

undertaken mundane projects such as advising the mayor on possible applications of solar energy for town buildings and imaginative ones such as studying the use of a nearby abandoned quarry as a heat storage pond to provide warmth for town buildings. It has also been able to point out to the mayor of another town that rather than waiting for a multimillion-dollar federal grant to solve a waste-disposal problem, the town could for a fraction of the cost begin switching new construction to the use of composting toilets and even subsidizing the retrofitting of older homes to the same technology.

There is in every town talent and imagination. Coupled with conscious and uninhibited desire to brainstorm possibilities, that talent and imagination can be a useful part of a public policy which itself could become aware of the technological choices underlying political choices. If those technological choices are not known, the political choices will be restricted, perhaps dangerously and counterproductively, to conventional and even failed paths.

There are no legal, moral, *or* technical reasons why a town or a neighborhood should not add technological awareness, research, and innovation to its public spaces and discussions. All that is lacking is the decision to do it and the will to work at it.

In times such as these it would certainly seem prudent to make the decision and exercise the will. Certainly, conventional attitudes have gone about as far as they can go.

The goals of a community technology group and its projects should include the demystification of technology so that instead of seeming a mysterious force it can become part of everyday life, including public life and policy. If not demystified it can easily become the master of and not the servant of those policies.

Another goal should be to challenge all of the claimed economies of scale that find many communities despairing of being self-reliant or being able to control their own destinies to any extent at all.

Overall, the goal should be to demonstrate the possibilities of technology in direct service to human needs in local settings, either in urban neighborhoods or in a town or county.

The group should, beyond demonstrations, gather useful information relating to technology which is both usable by and useful for communities of people—technology which, although possibly sophisticated in concept, is low in impact on the environment, and low also in demands upon the fixed or nonrenewable resources of the communities.

The uncomfortable feeling about technology that has kept so many of us afraid of it, aloof from it, or just plain frustrated by it derives from a situation that was brilliantly and succinctly described by Paul and Percival Goodman in their book *Communitas:*

Technology is a sacred cow left strictly to [unknown] experts, as if the form of the industrial machine did not profoundly affect every person; and people are remarkably superstitious about it. They think it is more efficient to centralize, whereas it is usually more inefficient. . . . They imagine as an article of faith that big factories must be more efficient than smaller ones; it does not occur to them, for instance, that it is cheaper to haul machines and parts than to transport workmen.

Indeed, they are outraged by good-humored demonstrations of [Ralph] Borsodi that, in hours and minutes of labor, it is probably cheaper to grow and can your own tomatoes than to buy them at the supermarket, not to speak of the quality. Here once again we have the inevitable irony of history; industry, invention, scientific method, have opened new opportunities, but just at the moment of opportunity, people have become ignorant of specialization and superstitious of science and technology, so that they no longer know what they want, nor do they dare to command it. The facts are exactly like the world of Kafka: a person has every kind of electrical appliance in his home, but he is balked, cold-fed, and even plunged into darkness because he no longer knows how to fix a faulty connection.

The curative, as described by Dr. John Blair, is a "new industrial revolution." It is a revolution of new techniques, new tools, and new materials that allow for decentralized technology that is relatively simple to use and inexpensive to operate—and accessible to understanding by all of us and, therefore, to development, deployment, and maintenance by all of us. Dr. Blair says of the materials involved that they "are neither labor intensive, nor capital intensive. They are knowledge intensive."

Yet, as the Goodmans pointed out twenty-five years ago, people have become more uneasy, insecure, and even superstitious about technology. Today's headlined debates about energy shortages, food prices, and housing problems are phrased in terms of national and international reference. The problems are not considered, as I certainly feel they should be, in terms of reference to our own local resources and to the possibilities of local solutions. Instead, even as the major institutions continue to display their inability to solve problems, we continue to turn to them. Only, however, when people turn away from them does there seem any real hope. And more and more people are turning and seeing that hope.

There is a growing realization that community technology (or what others call "alternative," "low impact," "centrifugal," or "liberatory" technology) can revive our communities, raise—not lower!—our standard of living, and give people a new sense and reality of regaining control over factors which we know crucially affect our lives and well-being but which we have in the recent past been content to leave to the control of others—the experts. In virtually every city today, in many towns, and even in many of those fortresses of conventional wisdom, the colleges, there are projects centering on some sort of alternative technology and often on some sort of alternative social organization at the same time.

If there is an element lacking to turn this disposition into a movement of genuine social impact, it is simply the element of consciously linking the work of alternative technologists to the problems of specific and existing communities rather than seeing the work as appropriate mostly to experimental communities, homesteads, and the like.

A way to do this is to imbed the work in the community and not confine it to exotic areas or atmospheres; to keep the work centered upon practical, immediate, and material possibilities rather than "futurist" musings; to assure that work relies upon interaction with the community, upon being part of the community rather than being an exterior force telling the community what it should do from a position of elite knowledge and superior taste.

It is not enough to search for new possibilities in community technology. Information and working models must also be provided so that community people and groups, or entire communities, may themselves adopt and adapt the technology best suited to their purposes.

Two major goals, therefore, emerge for a community technology group, as I see it: the accumulation of and the assurance of easy access to information concerning technological options

79

and impacts, and the construction of demonstration models of technologies that solve as many problems as possible while causing as few as possible.

It is a major attribute of what has come to be called alternative technology that it is concerned at the outset with the problems that a technological fix can cause as well as the ones it can solve. It is a mark of commercial or state technology that is concentrates on *neither* as strongly as it does on the matter of the extent to which the technology can strengthen the *institution's* position. And even when it does have to take into account problem solving of a more general nature, it virtually never seems inclined to consider subsidiary effects (the connection between the fumes of combustion engines and cigarettes, and emphysema, for instance).

The specific projects that can emerge from thinking about community technology could begin with either the software of the information function or the hardware of the demonstration function. Circumstances will suggest which way to go.

If there is in the community a problem that sticks out like a sore thumb, then the demonstration approach might seem most attractive as a start. Suppose that in a small town or an urban neighborhood the problem that bothers many people is the sanitary sewer system. It may be overloaded, obsolete, or leaking. A group interested in alternative technology might have the information available to see composting toilets as a cheap, sensible, hygienic solution—and propose a demonstration. The demonstration should keep the group together, giving it plenty of shared activity, should give it familiarity in the community, should tempt others to join in, and, if the final demonstration is successful, make it apparent that an ongoing activity would be good for the community and feasible *in* the community.

Need to heat a public building and high costs might combine in another instance to suggest a demonstration of solar energy as a first activity.

On the other hand, if the formation of the community

technology group derives internally, in response to the individual interests of a few people in the community, then it might be best to emphasize the information function at the outset. Our own group in a small town in West Virginia began that way. Its meetings were for a year simply show-and-tell, info-swapping sessions. Demonstration projects came later—with the design of a heat-storage system for a local vocational school greenhouse and then with the building of exhibit models of alternative energy systems for a public display in connection with the first observance of national Sun Day.

The functions of information for a community technology group might well be patterned after the very ones some of us outlined when establishing our first group in Washington, D.C.

—To gather, catalogue, and aid in the interpretation of existing information relevant to the continuing projects of the group. In addition, this activity would prepare a base for the community's use of technology and for the evaluation of future projects.

—To survey original research aimed at adaptations of scientific and engineering knowledge and techniques to the sort of community-oriented technology which is the special concern of the group. (The group itself should make a special effort to keep up with "outside" technological developments which might be scaled for community use. Despite the blueprinted scale of a particular advance, there is always the chance that it contains some effective principle or design which is easily translated to a community rather than institutional scale.)

—To disseminate the information that is developed or discovered, not only to the local community of which the group is part, but also to other groups working along similar lines elsewhere, thus opening and maintaining a flow of information and a steady stimulation of fresh thought.

The group, either on its own or in association with the local public library, a school, or some other familiar and dependable (and open-minded) existing facility, would probably be well advised to establish a library of material relevant to community technology. The emphasis might vary according to whether the group is in a big-city neighborhood or in a small town, close to a university or remote, or in a rural area, where separately, Future Farmers of America, the Grange, Ruritan, 4-H, or other similar groups might want to cooperate in establishing the library.

The library should include books, articles, and reports from several areas of science, engineering, and the practical arts. A temptation might be to emphasize the journals and reports of other like-minded groups. Their work, of course, is important and appropriate. But conventional journals should not be overlooked or undervalued. *Technology Review,* for instance, which is the regular journal of the Massachusetts Institute of Technology, has an actual and often-stated bias against decentralized technology and yet its superb reportage of a wide variety of technical innovations is constant grist for the mills of innovative alternative experimenters. Just because MIT thinks of every development in terms of corporate activity is no reason why you should.

There is a similar comment to be made about such standard basic journals as *Scientific American* and *Science,* the journal of the American Association for the Advancement of Science. *Scientific American* often carries the first generally understandable news of important technological advances which have obvious implications for community technology: no-till farming and trickle irrigation would be recent examples. *Science,* on the other hand, not only covers the upper reaches but also has reported favorably on alternative and decentralized technology experiments, including our own in Washington, D.C.

Of very particular interest should be pop magazines such as *Popular Science, Popular Mechanics,* and *Mechanix Illustrated.* The fact of the matter is that *Popular Science* over the past few years has had probably the most complete coverage of such alternative technologies as solar energy of any publication in the land, barring only such specialized ones as *Solar Energy*

Digest and *Alternative Sources of Energy*. The craftsmanlike approach and do-it-yourself emphasis of the pop magazines make them especially attractive to community technology experimenters.

The most natural publications for the library will be the ones that have actually identified themselves with appropriate or low-impact technology. (It is simply because they are so natural that I would personally urge the community technologist to attend to a search of other "straight" publications before loading up with tried and true familiars.)

Mother Earth News, Organic Gardening and Farming, Co-Evolution Quarterly, and that British masterpiece *Undercurrents* are the kinds of publications that probably have turned more people to thinking of alternative technologies than any others. They remain important and standard in their field. Regional publications, such as Portland, Oregon's, wide-ranging and, to my mind, outstanding, publication, *Rain*, should also have an important place in the library. Another such publication would be *North Country Anvil*, from Millville, Minnesota.

Of special interest and significance is *Self-Reliance*, the newsletter of the Institute for Local Self-Reliance, 1919 18th Street N.W., Washington, D.C. 20009. Not only is the institute's publication a fine one, the institute itself is a good active example of community technology information gathering and demonstration. Although the institute itself does not identify with just a single community, its work is usually with community groups, such as a composting project it is conducting with people in the South Bronx, or various gardening and energy projects in the Washington area.

Community activities of a general nature that can grow out of the technology group's information gathering could also include the showing of films. During the celebration of Sun Day, our group in West Virginia was able to collect three hours' worth of films on solar energy, for free, to be shown in the town. Films are often a good way of opening the door to any discussion. They are not, however, in any way a substitute for regular public meetings in which neighbor-to-neighbor talking builds ideas and a community of interest that cannot be provided by simply being a spectator at a film showing.

Somewhere, one community technology group with just the right combination of skill and energy might take on an information function which has always seemed to me to have considerable potential value. That would be a regular review of patents to spot those which might have application to community-scale technological interests.

A similar, perhaps even more ambitious and therefore usefully shared and decentralized, sort of information activity would be to keep in close touch with college engineering, architecture, science, and agriculture departments to spot activities with community applications. Few such departments are interested in such applications, but the work they do may have precisely such applications whether they care for them to or not. Community technologists should not overlook this possibly rich lode of informational ore. Cooperating community technology groups could parcel out such survey work, tackling a set of schools in each of their areas.

For any community technology group near a college or university there is a special challenge in keeping in touch with technical faculties and students. First, there is always the chance that a school, particularly a land grant school, might be talked into actively sharing information and skills—and even tools—with a nearby community. The resistance will, of course, be strong, since most schools see themselves as serving not communities but corporations. Nevertheless, colleges and universities do exist in or near communities, some faculty members have paid at least lip service to the fact, and the thing could be gently pushed by a community technology group. Nothing to lose. Certainly, for a community college or a vocational school the link-up should be natural and practical. That it would be in every case desirable is a point community technologists might want to keep making.

A tie-in that falls somewhere between the informational and the demonstrational would be with small businesses in the area, specifically shops and garages and with such professionals as civil engineers, architects, and builders. The small business description is emphasized because of the regrettable but nonetheless real difficulty experienced with virtually any big business with a plant in the area. First, the community is only of "tactical" interest, a sort of necessary nuisance, more to be held at bay than to be treated as an actual friend and neighbor. Also, few decisions of any value can be made at the local level in such plants, so that even a request to make available for community use discarded materials or tools becomes a long, tortured process with the head office. This shouldn't rule out cooperation, it should simply put it into perspective. It should be kept in mind that the interests of a community and of any absentee-owned business are unlikely to be the same. The number of big business "good neighbors" who pack up and leave a community at the rise or drop of a profit point should remind everyone of the very limited possibilities of similar interests between a community of people and a big corporation. Its community, after all, lives in the board room and the posh suburbs and simply is not and never will be just folks in the neighborhood.

With truly local plants and craft firms, however, there can be identities of interest and, perhaps, sharings of skill, information, and even tools. Turning over depreciated tools for community use is one area that might be fruitfully explored, just as might the acquisition of government surpluses, through a town's offices.

Although it might seem that there would be an inevitable clash of interests between the public service emphasis of a community technology group and the profit necessity of the small business, there is nothing that actually demands such a conflict. If a community can in its public spaces and decisions use the best and most suitable technology, the savings and advantages accrue to all. It should ease, not exacerbate, relations with small businesses and with property owners in general by easing off the upward spiral of taxation which is often associated with using high-cost, brute-force conventional technological answers to local problems rather than seeking native local-resource solutions.

Where there are conflicts between a public service and a profit approach, there is also a good opportunity for adding a new dimension to community awareness and discussions. Certainly the community should discuss and in the long run decide *which* areas of activity are best served by which of the approaches. There is certainly nothing sacred about either approach, the competitive profitable one or the cooperative public service one.

A good case can be made for the fact that any community service could be carried on by either means. Some towns do have private profit-making fire departments; they work well. On the other hand, most communities have volunteer fire departments, and they work well. Larger towns, of course, have professional departments, paid out of taxes. They work well too. The decision should be prudential, not theological.

A very important underlying strength of the community technology group could be to bring into the social forum the sort of common-sense or even engineering approach to public problems that would show that reasonable people can make reasonable choices about how to get things done, without having to be constricted to either ritual acceptance of what has been or fantasized fear of what could be.

After all, in deciding whether the town wants to operate, say, a golf course or a factory or a power station, the arguments should involve how the *people* involved want to live. If you think that Way A serves your purposes best then that's the way. If Way B does it for another bunch, then that's *their* way. Some communities, for example, have turned down the almost inevitably lower rates of a municipal power station because they simply do not want to have to bother about adding power management to the roster of civic interests. They'd rather pay a higher rate and let someone else do all the worrying. Fair enough, and certainly more sensible than turning down such a proposition simply because it *is* public rather than private. The opposite is also true, of course. To pick a way only because it *is* public, whether it ends up making your life better or not, would be stupid.

Questions such as those, however, keep coming up in any community technology effort and serve as a very useful reminder of something that should never be forgotten. There are *two* parts to the phrase "community technology." It is not all gadgets. The gadgets—the technology—are simply there as the support for the first part—the community. The purpose of any human activity, I have come to feel, should be the enhancement of the lives of the people involved. That sort of betterment may have many definitions. To some it will mean securing a bedrock foundation for a deeply loved and unchanging way of living. The Amish are such a community. To others it may mean a place of kaleidoscopic possibility, and many an artistic community is like that. To most it probably will mean trade-offs and combinations of such things, a community in which there is the security of shared values and ways of living, some excitement, probably through cultural expressions, or maybe sports, and so forth. No matter how people want to live, they still must devise *means* to do it. Even a decision to live stark naked in a grove of trees would require some attention to climate, to bark scrapes and the alleviation thereof, to silvaculture, and to some sort of agreement with surrounding communities to whom your decision might seem vile or laughable, or both. In short, a decision to live a certain way has a practical dimension no matter how airy.

It is in approaching this practical side that the gadgets are important and that a community technology group will make exciting and noteworthy contributions—but those contributions will be made only in light of that most basic of all considerations, the social notion of how people want to live together. And again, just because some of the technology that a

87

community technologist might come up with is highly imaginative or even astonishing, sight should not be lost of the fact that the underlying social decision may be nowhere near so dramatic. For most people it may simply be to continue living roughly the way they do in the existing neighborhood or town. Community technology is undertaken, in all cases of which I am aware, in the knowledge that even to do that in these days of social and resource crunches may well require some very fast technological footwork, that the technologies of massive size and institutional centralism are no longer reassuring of real possibilities today, no more than are the social institutions of great scale and centralism which have presided over most of the upheavals which we now see as undesirable. In other words, the big-scale central authorities have created more problems than solutions. The community technologist must hope to do the reverse and must depend on being a part of the community for a good deal of the common sense which can help prevent massive mistakes, repetition of past error, and bureaucratic insistence on form versus substance.

Perhaps just a good beginning, eschewing internal hierarchy and starting in a neighborly rather than institutional spirit, helps. Our group in West Virginia began simply on the basis of a half dozen posted notices and a brief item in the local paper suggesting that people get together at the public library on a particular night to discuss such things as solar energy, water power, new ways of organizing work, gardening, wood energy, and so forth. About thirty people showed up the first night and that has become a fairly average monthly attendance with more than a hundred people seeming to feel themselves to be members. All of the meetings are announced in the paper, results are also publicized, such as indicating who is starting to build a windmill, who wants advice on steam engines, and so forth. The local Chamber of Commerce directs people interested in such things to the meetings. The group has no officers. Its newsletter is done on an ad hoc basis by volunteers, although Therese Hess sort of coordinates it because she usually types it. Dues are not asked but a hat is passed from time to time to defray newsletter mailing and paper. This has been going on now since early 1977. One result has been that the group and its meetings are now fairly well accepted in the area as dependable sources of information on alternative technologies. And even now the group is negotiating with the area's splendid Vo-Tech center to use its facilities for a more formal information system and to open room for some courses in solar energy and perhaps later in the whole range of things that could be associated with community technology.

Continuing then with things we are either doing, want to do, or can see some use in someone else doing, there are two offshoots of the information function of a community technology group that might be useful and revealing.

One, which we earnestly hope to begin in our own area soon, is to make a good and full inventory of the productive facilities which already exist in the public space of both the towns and the county.

To understand the possibilities of sharing of things which are of a technological nature, you might be well advised to know whether you are actually doing some of it already. Among other things it brings a familiar touch to something which otherwise might seem unfamiliar and thus threatening.

There is a town surveyor, for instance. His office, you could say, already is a publicly shared and financed center for the application of trigonometric and geometric functions. Also, there is likely to be some first-class equipment in such an office. Applications? The office and the equipment might be helpful in siting wind generation experiments, in studying stream configurations and water power sites.

Road repair and building equipment represents a power-house of tools. The community technology group anxious to study shared or community heat-storage facilities or to build a demonstration earth-insulated house could find vital tools in the town garage.

In urban neighborhoods there are also possibilities with city equipment, using some, for instance, to bulldoze lots for community gardens, or borrowing help from the fire department to mount a rooftop collector.

The inventory can bring to light the crucial community technology points that tools are important and that they may be shared on a community basis without in any way ideologically or morally fencing off the possibility of other types of sharing, using, or owning!

To continue, printing equipment is another item of interest, of course, to any group hoping to disseminate information. Sometimes there are lab facilities maintained to test water supplies. Then, of course, there are maintenance shops in general. Who really knows the tools of a town until he or she looks carefully? And who knows the possibilities of sharing and extending their use until a serious question along those lines is asked?

It is possible that the school systems and libraries will have concentrations of tools to make the community technologist leap with joy. School labs do have equipment that, if the community technology group can share in paying for, might be used on a community basis after school hours. On the other hand, there may be instances where a community technology proposal and its exploration might itself be a superb way of teaching skills to school classes. The public library's main resource is a trained ability to help in working out information retrieval systems and perhaps even providing space for information storage.

County extension agents should be considered prime potential resources of a community technology effort, and lest the fact be overlooked, these agents with their access to information and often with available mechanical equipment are also present in big cities. In Washington D.C., where most people never even suspected that a county agent would exist, one certainly did and very helpfully provided a tiller for some of our original community gardening efforts.

There is no limit to where a community technology group

should go for help. Recently our group received informational assistance of a first-class sort from people at NASA's high-technology Goddard Space Flight Center. Some folks there, working on a new heat concentrator for a solar heating system, actually came to visit us with a model and with helpful advice. Even a police laboratory could offer a possibility for a community technologist. If the lab has a spectrometer, you might talk your way into some time on the machine to analyze soil samples suspected of heavy metal concentrations which can occur in areas near highways or in smogged city lots.

Whenever the community technology group reaches out for help, it should remind itself that the emphasis is as much on community as technology and that fascination with the gadgets should never overpower fealty to the neighborhood.

Variations of the sort of surveying of tools suggested in the town inventory would involve finding out everything possible about the same things in other sectors.

A community skill-resource inventory should be useful. It would involve a systematic door-to-door canvassing of the entire community (the way a dedicated church goes about it, for instance) to discover what social and tutorial skills are held by people in the community. At the same time you could raise the question of the extent to which the people are willing to commit those skills to community projects.

Churches, by the way, can always be important allies in any community venture, just as they can be overpowering foes. In rural areas today, many ministers are more willing than ever to experiment with new social and technical forms. Shared activities have always been an important part of rural and small-town churches, with cooperative helping-hand projects being constant and familiar. Perhaps today it would not seem bizarre at all for a church intent on helping a family in the congregation to think about a solar hot water heater where they might have thought of an electric one a few years ago. There is, of course, one obvious attribute of the solar device that might appeal to some of the congregation. They could build it, thus carrying a step further the notion of the Lord helping those who help themselves.

In making the community skill inventory, it should be possible also to survey tools and resources—from hobby-centered basement shops, to heavy-duty farm repair sheds, from special libraries to the person who just likes to store old papers or magazines, to basements or garages or sheds full of scrap wood or metal that someone is keeping "just in case." Maybe the community technology group and the experiments could be "the case."

Too often the resources of a community are viewed only in money terms or in some statistical way. A community technology survey of the sort outlined above would certainly expand the narrowness of that older concept and point to what in the long run might be the richest of all community resources and the only sure gauge of its self-reliance: the shared knowledge and skills and tools of its residents.

Another sort of survey that would look at present resources but also concentrate more than any of the other activities so far suggested on future possibilities would be a community productivity study.

The community technology group for a study of this importance and depth probably would want to involve as many other groups in the community as possible.

Such a study would keep in mind two points in particular, points which could be seen as the pivots or hinges for the study. First, existing decentralized technologies—including cybernated machine tools, minicomputers, biological production of complex chemical substances through DNA research, high-grade plastics molding, electronics generally, on-site alternative energy production, intensive gardening—beg to be studied carefully by communities of human beings no matter the mass production, central authority direction of big business and big government. Communities of people obviously need to begin to think of their own well-being in their own terms rather than being carried along by the momentum of big institutional plans.

Second, in studying the future and the tools available to shape it with, the community needs to think seriously and democratically about just how it wants to live in the near and the long term and how it might best get on with doing it. And just as the study of available technologies should be undertaken with an open mind and without the restrictions of conventional wisdom (which at the moment keeps saying that you should let the experts and the big boys do it), so should the study of how a community wants to live. The study should not begin with a pessimistic notion of not being able to change anything. There is nothing to lose at all if the discussion begins instead with the idea that we can do *anything*. It is better to discover restrictions as you go along than to never explore at all and thus risk never discovering even the smallest hopeful possibility.

Many a civic group or business group or service group in many a town has found it useful to plan for the future. How can it hurt? Many also find that a lot of the planning is just an exercise in futility because somehow "practical" matters always grind it down. The suggestion in the approaches mentioned is that by studying tools and possibilities and dreams at the same time and always keeping them linked as tightly as you can, there is a better chance of emerging with something that *is* practical. The dream would have a material base as well as a social base. It is founded on productive reality even though it rises to heights of speculative Utopianism.

Imagine, to consider just one detail of what such a study might encompass, what it would mean for a town, through some sort of community garden space, to provide all the food to alleviate the hunger of welfare clients in the area, rather than using cash resources to buy the food from distant suppliers. A social dimension: What is the effect of alleviating some welfare needs, such as food, through the work efforts of those welfare clients able to assist in the gardens? Would prisoners be better served and the community better guarded if they worked in a community garden project? What about gardens and education? Year round? What about putting some garden

93

space into greenhouse areas? How do you plan such green-houses? Hmmmm. Maybe the community technology group should be working on that in conjunction with some local plumbers and florists. But mightn't all that community effort divert money from local merchants or craftsmen? For one thing, most money for welfare food is spent at stores that buy from remote areas and whose profits are siphoned off to other communities. Any threat to local incomes needs seriously to be considered, of course. Perhaps if new ways of doing things permitted a lowering of taxes, the first benefits should go to any neighbor adversely affected by the activity. It *is* an important point and one which the community itself should discuss and decide. Suggestions such as I am mak-ing should never be considered more than suggestions and never should be considered substitutes for the neighborhood, community discussions, which alone make a community tech-nology worthwhile in the long run.

Specific demonstration projects and activities that might interest a community technology group should focus on the heart of the matter, which is community, as well as the hands of the matter—tools. The idea is not to tinker just for the love of tinkering, but to tinker for the love of being a good neighbor and wanting to live a good life in a good place on a healthy earth.

Community technology, information sharing, and demonstration are responses to facts. The way we live must be based upon material reality, upon the way we work in part, upon the way we use land and resources in part, upon the way we make decisions in part. What we do and the tools with which we do it are part of a process, not separate things, off, isolated, and compartmentalized. Finally, the way we live need not be dependent upon uncontrollable forces either of history, economics, politics, institutional pressure, or even conventional wisdom. It need not be if we *want* to, and will take those actions which will enable us to define our desires, see our situation clearly, envision ways to accomplish what we want, and clearly and in practical terms base our desires upon available resources and either potential or available tools and techniques.

With that in mind, and with the community technologist defined basically as a person who 1) agrees and 2) is willing to work at it, using or acquiring skills to make something possible, projects can abound. Here are a few:

A shared machine shop might be a useful demonstration since it aims at both areas of the community technology concern: ways of working together *and* tools. It doesn't say that all work and all tools must be shared; it simply says that some tools and some work (community research work in this case) may *usefully* be shared.

The machine shop should have enough basic tools, both hand and power, to make the building of demonstration models or test facilities a practical and everyday activity. The shared shop might just be part of some other public facility, used in its off-hours. Or the shop might be separate and stocked with cast-off industrial tools, with tools bought from government surplus through the local school system. Or a community technology group might just go ahead and do it themselves. Work can, of course, be done as well in home shops or in commercial shops of people who like the community technology approach. Results should be fine, but the participants would miss the creative challenge of the *shared* shop.

Although it might not be immediately evident, such a machine shop probably has more significance in an inner-city neighborhood than in a small town or rural area. For one thing, shop and even laboratory equipment is commonplace in small towns and rural areas. People already have habits and practices of self-reliance that make this likely.

In the inner city, generations of dependence upon politicians to solve problems and on welfare to end poverty have dulled a good deal of skill and sharing and any other sort of emphasis on material, as opposed to administrative, activity.

For inner-city residents, the shared machine shop might be a sensible and practical doorway to the neglected world of productivity, as well as being a base for community experimentation and demonstration.

Thinking of such a shared workshop in an inner city, you can think of its use also for the maintenance of appliances and other household goods whose replacement might represent a real economic burden in the neighborhood and whose myster-

96

ies might be an important part in the feeling of helplessness that many inner-city people develop.

Such a function in a small town or rural area might not be nearly so appropriate since there are fix-it shops aplenty and they probably represent an honest and useful part of the community's existing economy. Rural people are usually handy.

In either case there might be similar projects that the machine shop could undertake beyond the building of demonstration models and other regular community technology tasks. The machine shop could regularly redesign cast-off items into useful ones. Discarded refrigerators, for instance, suggest an infinity of new uses, from fish tanks, after removing doors, to numerous small parts as each discarded one is stripped for its components, which include small compressors, copper tubing, heat transfer arrays, and so on. The same goes for washing machines. In small towns a nice bonus of recycling such things is that the local landfill or other disposal project doesn't have the problem of disposing of these relatively large hunks of junk; and that's all they *are* unless given a new life by the community technologists!

Similar in spirit to the shared machine shop could be a shared warehouse. Everyone knows the agony of having to throw something away even though instinct says that someday it will be needed. But space does us all in—apartment dwellers immediately, homesteaders finally.

A community decision to share a space in which discarded materials can be stored, categorized, and made easily available is a decision to use an otherwise wasted resource, to be ingenious, and to take back into the hands of the community an active role in making decisions about industrial processes. In this case, of course, the decisions are made at the end of the process, where usually the trash collector and the dump operator are the only players. But, it has been my observation that when people begin to take a new active part in any segment of their lives, it becomes a self-feeding passion, urging a person on for more and more responsibility, more and more self-reliance, more and more action as a whole person and not merely as a spectator.

The shared warehouse—which might also have some impact on the community's welfare problems, if wanted—should collect a trove of bits and pieces of building materials, no matter whether in the inner city or in a rural area or small town. There always seems to be a bundle of wood at the end of any project that is too good to burn, too junky to sell, and too insignificant to store. Put a lot of those bundles together and the picture changes to more and more practical possibilities of building materials for the public space.

Spare parts are fair game for the community warehouse. Thus it can serve as a parts cabinet for the community technology experimenters. Where might the warehouse be located? Unused public space is always a good place to start the search—basements, unused equipment sheds, or abandoned buildings, which could present a dual challenge of community rehabilitation work plus providing community technology space.

Fantasy, perhaps, but a local vocational school might even want to operate a community junkyard as a way to train people in the imaginative and creative skills of operating a good junkyard.

A problem common to many communities is the plight of more resources leaving than coming back in. This is particularly true with national marketing systems that draw resources toward a few centers rather than encouraging a scattering among many communities. The shared work space and the shared warehouse space involve a community in taking a first look at this problem at a homely and nonideological level. It could be hoped that after the process is begun it will continue until the community is prepared to discuss every aspect of its resource base and its shared interests in regard to it.

For many communities these days the first and most obvious place to start any community technology demonstration or experiment is in the area of energy. My own prejudice is that food comes first, as indicated throughout these comments. A good look at a community's food base, it seems to me, would be more enlightening in many ways than a look at the energy base. Nevertheless, energy is obviously on more minds today than food. Experiments and demonstrations in alternative sources of energy are a quick entryway to the interests of most communities. The most obviously intriguing part of it is solar energy. Fortunately, it is the part most susceptible to community technology demonstration, even in northern climes.

Of solar energy projects, one of the most immediately productive and economically feasible is hot water heating. Even in southern climates, where solar space-heating devices might lie idle most of the year, hot water heaters would perk away full-time. Furthermore, the use of hot water heating, particularly in schools, might be an item of substantial community interest from a purely economic point of view.

Community technology groups, cooperating with local officials, should be able easily to make convincing demonstrations of the feasibility of solar hot water heating, starting perhaps with out-of-the-way installations such as in road- or building-maintenance shops, then moving on to more prominent places. Whereas the community technology group might be biting off a bit too much to offer to install solar space-heating collectors on a local school building, they might be able quickly and easily to do it for a sheriff's substation or a road-maintenance office—or a dog pound. Inner-city opportunities are as numerous as the buildings in the neighborhood.

My own feeling is that the what or the where of the solar experiment is not as important as the process of *doing* it wherever and however. It begins that process crucial to a community technology outlook in which you feel that new answers can be found for old problems and that you and your neighbors can find them and apply them.

In most community technology ventures it is quite probable, my experience has shown, that individual experimenters themselves will have taken the lead in designing and installing innovative systems of some sort, so when an opportunity for public demonstrations comes along, there will be some practical experience on hand as well as plenty of theoretical knowledge. Also, in looking at answers such as solar heating, the community technology group will be an important agency for convincing tradespeople and craftspeople in the area that they are, as they definitely *are*, already engaged in matters with direct possibilities of conversion to solar energy. Sheet metal workers have most of the skills needed to install good solar hot air systems. A little brush-up on physics—helped by the community technology group meetings!—and the sheet metal worker *is* a solar worker. It is the same with plumbers and liquid transfer solar systems. Everyone involved in building supplies or construction has skills that are directly applicable. And bankers have skills required for financing! Money also is a tool.

Storage of solar heat is a prime area of experimentation for any community technology group. In our area, large unused and abandoned quarries represent a resource we will be investigating to see if the caverns or ponds of the quarries could be used for community-wide heat storage or, sequentially, for "cold storage" (air conditioning).

In regard to solar energy, however, the community technology group has another responsibility and opportunity. It should keep very close tabs on the development both of chemical and mechanical energy storage systems and also on the development of devices for direct conversion of solar energy to electrical energy. The speed with which photovoltaic cells for direct conversion are dropping in cost makes me strongly suspect that we are on the edge of an energy revolution more far-reaching than any we have ever known. Should that revolution have a moving effect only at the most centralized and remote levels of social authority, we may be in for real trouble if an energy source that could be dramatically liberating is instead bureaucratically or economically shackled to the purposes of either big business or big government.

Community technology groups working at the local level would do well to keep their friends, their town officials, and their inner-city groups closely advised on the possibilities of using photovoltaic energy *before* it becomes chained to one or another corporate interest, either government or private.

Wind energy is the next most feasible demonstration area for a community technology group. Whether in the city or in the country, wind is everywhere.

In the original outline of the community technology group that we established in Washington, D.C., there is a still interesting and succinct wind energy proposal:

The wind power project will investigate a number of different aspects of wind-generated energy: high and low speed mills for electrical generation and pumping; speed-up effect of shrouded mills and natural urban wind tunnels; effects of placement of units; effects of wind generator "fields" (what is the environmental effect of having a large number of units in a relatively small area?). We will work with propeller, turbine, and Savonius systems, with both professional and "funk" (recycled junk) technologies. The units will be developed around the neighborhood with cooperating groups, in order to get a wider range of feedback.

The initial phase of this project will be data gathering. We will deploy a series of recording anemometers around the neighborhood, at a variety of altitudes, in order to develop a suitable picture of the local microclimate, to guide us in mill site selection. We will then build a series of small (under 12-foot diameter), relatively low powered (under one kilowatt) mills, to investigate several questions simultaneously: blade shrouding systems; control feathering and braking systems; battery, hydrogen, gravity, and compressed air power storage; and turbines and Savonius rotors for low wind speed applications.

We will later apply what we learn from the small mill experiments to the construction of a larger (two kilowatt) plant. Barring unforeseen setbacks, within a year we hope to have a refined design for, and proceed with, the construction of a series of one and two kilowatt units. The capital cost of such units will be about $250–$300 per kilowatt installed capacity. This figure may seem high in comparison with the $125–$130 figure offered for conventional steam generating plants, but consider: (1) that the steam plant figure does not include environmental costs of thermal and atmospheric pollution; (2) that proponents of nuclear generating plants (which, we are told, are the wave of the future) are at present projecting a cost of about $300 per kilowatt installed capacity, and that estimate climbs every year; and (3) that operating expenses, although initially higher than conventional costs, are less likely to increase than conventional costs, deplete no resources, and show every indication of decreasing as experience increases—a factor no longer claimable for conventional power sources.

For many small towns and rural areas there is a special and growing interest in the use of wood as a fuel. Vermont has made it a state priority.

Community technology groups can certainly help out with this. First of all, they can make sure that they and their neighbors are really up to date on what's available commercially in the way of good wood-burning equipment. Evaluations of such equipment are important but so far hard to come by. But assuming that people scattered through a lot of towns are indeed buying a lot of brand-new wood stoves, and hoping that an interest in community technology springs up around the country, community technology groups could test whatever stove they might have available in a friend's home, then swap the information with other groups that might be testing some other design.

Community technology groups should also consider original designs and in keeping with the overall spirit should keep in mind the possibility that a good original design could be the basis for a community business or co-op, or even a town industry.

The stove is just part of the wood-burning process, however. Any community technology group has its work cut out for it in discussing and envisioning and then demonstrating novel ways of growing wood, perhaps on a community basis, cutting it, splitting it, drying it (a solar task?), and then dividing it for use. Also, they might want to consider the fact that heat from wood is a next-door neighbor to heat from, say, agricultural wastes and even certain industrial wastes. Could utilization of the wastes be useful in the community? Would it also provide a base not only for a new energy source but for a new productive outlet for the town's manpower?

Community technologists should never stop with just one question if they can help it. Or settle for just one answer!

Specialized vehicles are the sort of problem that particularly interests me, and they show the wide range of community technology possibilities in any community. Considerable public money is spent annually on cars and trucks. Often the money is spent buying specialized equipment which, although it will only seldom be used, is felt to be worth it. Some of that, surely, could be built locally.

In our neighborhood in Washington it was clear from a couple of weeks' study that one of the most important moving devices for the neighborhood would be a sort of self-propelled platform that could move heavy items of furniture for a few blocks, to take care of ordinary household moving needs or for community activities in which chairs, musical instruments, platforms, or such gear had to be moved a few blocks. An expensive pick-up truck would have been a waste of money. Our solution was to take the cheapest car we could get that was still operable, cut it down, mount a platform across its rear, leaving just a cockpit for the driver, and, lo and behold, we would have a very low cost moving platform.

Small towns might have similar problems. They also might have junk cars to dispose of—a happy juxtaposition of resource and possibility. Rural areas already are models of innovative vehicle design. Few farmers can resist designing new machines. We should all have this itch.

Also in cities there is need for community technology groups to design really good shopping carts capable of mounting curbs and steps, so that the elderly could do their shopping more easily. Of course there is just as much reason for the community technology group to think of ways for the elderly to organize their own gardens, for instance. Or to devise ways in which a neighborhood can simply stop itself from segregating the elderly into special ghetto conditions. Community technology is *not* just gadgets. Basically it's people—and about people.

And certainly food is a crucial "people issue." Again, from our original outline of community technology work in Washington, D.C., here are two specific proposals for food projects:

In the United States the quality of food is declining steadily, with highly processed foods accounting for an increasingly large segment of the American diet. As the USDA reports, the number of people eating "good" diets in this country has fallen to around 50 percent, with vitamin deficiency becoming commonplace, and the general health of the nation declining.

We will explore an approach that could go a long way toward alleviating both of these problems—decentralized food production. By taking advantage of unused basement and roof-top space, we hope to demonstrate that an urban community can provide itself with a steady supply of high quality fish protein and vitamin rich fresh vegetables, year-round, at low cost.

The initial projects in this area are hydroponic greenhouses and high-density trout culture. Coincident with these food raising projects, alternative community institutions for the equitable distribution of the food will be studied. Local food co-ops have already expressed an interest in being involved. The neighborhood organization also has begun discussions of the distribution question as well as pledging support to the food projects generally.

Hydroponics involves the growing of crops in a carefully controlled environment: soil (and thus the possibility of soil infestation and the need for fungicides) is eliminated and replaced with gravel, vermiculite, or similar substrate. Nutrients are supplied in a precisely formulated solution at specific intervals. Greenhouses are maintained at a temperature level, carbon dioxide concentration, and humidity suitable to encourage optimum growth. Yields produced by these techniques are dramatically higher than those from conventional agriculture, and year-round production is possible.

The feasibility of hydroponics is already well-established. Preliminary calculations (based on data from NASA and commercial and noncommercial growers) indicate that greenhouses covering 10 percent of the area of a city (or a fraction of its unused roof-top space) should provide the food needs of 18,200 people per square mile. (The density of Washington is about 13,000 per square mile.)

In the first year, we will construct and operate five greenhouses of 240 square feet each. About three-fourths of this space will be used to grow crops, including soybeans, tomatoes, squash, carrots, beets, greens, legumes, and possibly grains. The other 20 to 25 percent of the space will be devoted to research. We want to investigate, for a start, the economies of scale involved in choosing between family-size and block- or community-size facilities; the different varieties of nutrient solutions, including solutions prepared from composted "wastes"; comparison of the relative nutritional value of crops

104

produced; companion planting; simplified testing and control procedures so that units can be operated by individuals with little technical experience; and the possible problems entailed in dealing with a complex, interactive ecosystem in a reductionist setting. In addition, data gathered in these efforts will be used in the development of a longer-term project—integrated food, energy, and sewage systems for urban dwellings.

It is widely predicted that over the next three to five years there will be a dramatic decrease in supply and an increase in the price of seafood in the United States. This is expected to be a result of the dollar devaluation as well as the collapse of the domestic fishing industry and a decrease of the total world catch due to over-fishing by the modern, efficient European and Japanese fleets. This development would lead one to expect an increase in emphasis on domestic fish culture and, indeed, one is slowly taking place. The amount of fish produced by the industry, however, is minute in relation to the total seafood supply—something less than two percent of it. Most aquaculture operations are limited in their productive capacity by the amount of water available. A technology which is just now coming to fruition is water purification, which makes possible the use of large-scale water re-use systems.

The requirement, up until now, of large quantities of pure water for rearing fish has dictated that almost all commercial aquaculture sites be located at considerable distances from their most concentrated markets, the urban centers. Recent technological developments in water purification, however, suggest that it is possible to make such efficient use of the culture water that the situation can be reversed and that useful quantities of fish can be grown within the urban center itself, using water from the metropolitan domestic water supply but without adding any important strain on either the water supply or the sewerage system.

This movement of a food production facility into the city would immensely simplify the distribution of the perishable fresh fish to the concentrated market, would provide a new kind of industry in the city, and would provide some degree of control by the urban center over a component of its food supply.

As a first development and demonstration project, we propose to raise rainbow trout. Although this species has stringent water temperature requirements, there are many reasons for working with it. First, the starting materials—rainbow trout eggs or rainbow trout

105

fry—are available commercially throughout much of the year, allowing a nearly continuous year-round production of fish of marketable size. Second, efficient feed is commercially available. Third, more is known of the physiology and cultural requirements of the species than of any other fish. And fourth, the product has a nearly universal high acceptance.

The growth from "eyed" (fertilized) egg to table-size fish, generally an average of three-fourths of a pound, requires 12 months and about 1.2 pounds of feed. During this period the production is carried out in perhaps four different configurations of tanks of increasing sizes. In actual commercial production, the latter stages of growth would take place in a multiplicity of identical tanks. For the development and demonstration project, though, we will limit the throughput in the latter stages by using a maximum of four of the largest size experimental vessels (10 x 4 x 3 feet). This will give a continuous production at the rate of about 400 pounds of fish per month after the first cycle has been completed (12 months).

A facility of this size would permit a demonstration of the process in large enough equipment to remove all important questions of scale-up and would provide early-stage facilities for the production of, perhaps, 30 times the 400 pounds per month of the proposed demonstration unit if adequate later-stage facilities could be added.

For the demonstration units, we will use silo-type incubators and construct tanks of plywood and fiberglass with perhaps some of the larger vessels being made of ferro-cement. Each fish tank will have a biological ammonia converter for water purification and temperature will be controlled by insulating the tank room and using standard window-type air conditioners. Temperature will be maintained at 55 to 60 degrees F. and water usage, except under unusual circumstances, will be kept below 200 gallons per day.

Both of those experiments proved successful.

There is an inexhaustible array of demonstration possibilities for any community technology group; and even at your first meeting, should you and some friends decide to become such a group, you'll probably be able to fill a notebook with them.

Later, as the group enlarges its meetings and either goes to new people or draws them in, the possibilities should be endless and the trick will be in prudential priorities or in just seeing how much can be done before you collapse!

I would not even want to suggest how your community technology group might operate, internally or externally. I have suggested possibilities of purpose here and have emphasized several, but I would not want the suggestions or the emphasis to substitute in any way for your own inescapable responsibility, along with your friends, to make the basic decisions on your own, for your own purposes and in the light of your own knowledge of your own community.

If you want to organize such a group in the hope that you will become the newest business in town, making a good buck from advising on new technology—more power to you. Your work has got to be closer to the community and more responsible to its resources and needs than an outsider from a big business to whom your town is just another dot on an international map.

If you want to organize the group to look toward social ownership of basic productive needs, then more power to you also. Your work has got to be less regimenting than the plans of state socialists or even liberal traditional politicians.

If you want to organize the group to truly explore all sorts of human possibilities and do not even know now which you might prefer—more power to you also. Your work has got to be more libertarian than that of those who see the future as a game that can be played and predicted right now, to be fastened on us all tomorrow by elite decision.

My own interest is the responsibility of people to *be* responsible for their own lives and, with their neighbors, for their public space and actions. To sing their own songs. To make their own inventions. To be on stage and out of the audience. To love and not just yearn.

To build and not just envy. To light that candle which is so much better than cursing the darkness. To be as much as the human condition can sustain, rather than being only what a system can allow.

To be. To do. That is community technology.

107